Knitting Beyond the Basics

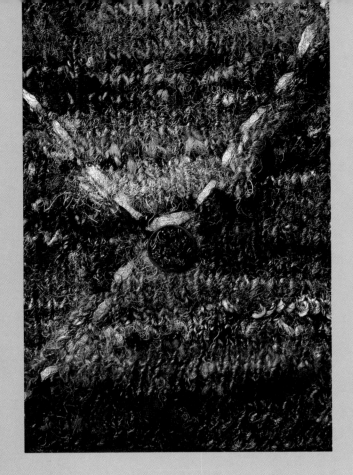

Knitting

Rebecca Lennox

Beyond the
Basics

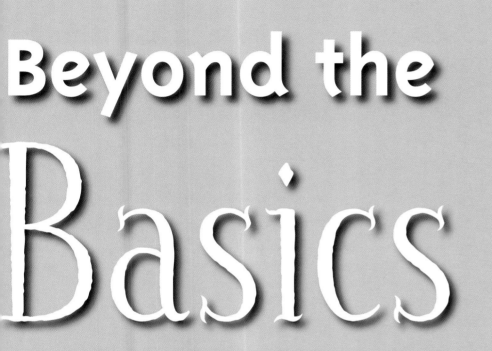

SKILL-BUILDING LESSONS and MUST-HAVE PROJECTS

Martingale®
& COMPANY

Knitting Beyond the Basics:
Skill-Building Lessons and Must-Have Projects
© 2007 by Rebecca Lennox

Martingale®
& COMPANY

Martingale & Company
20205 144th Ave. NE
Woodinville, WA 98072-8478 USA
www.martingale-pub.com

Credits

CEO: Tom Wierzbicki
Publisher: Jane Hamada
Editorial Director: Mary V. Green
Managing Editor: Tina Cook
Developmental Editor: Karen Costello Soltys
Technical Editor: Donna Druchunas
Copy Editor: Liz McGehee
Design Director: Stan Green
Illustrator: Robin Strobel
Cover and Text Designer: Stan Green
Photographer: Brent Kane

Printed in China
12 11 10 09 08 07   8 7 6 5 4 3 2 1

Library of Congress Cataloging-in-Publication Data
Library of Congress Control Number: 2007001141

ISBN: 978-1-56477-741-6

Mission Statement
Dedicated to providing quality products and service to inspire creativity.

Dedication

To Ben, Sue, and Maggie—the best parents a daughter could hope to have.

Acknowledgments

Special thanks to Tonie for organizing my chaos, Roberta for a little bit of everything, Debbie for knitting, Emily and Jacob for giving up their mom for a few months, and especially Dave for letting all my dreams come true.

Contents

Introduction ~ 8

Chapter 1
Knitting Basics ~ 9
Project: Mistake-Rib Afghan ~ 13

Chapter 2
Gauge, Shaping, and Finishing ~ 14
Project: Basic V-neck Cardigan ~ 22

Chapter 3
Edgings and Bands ~ 25
Project: Evening Jacket ~ 28
Project: Sideways Summer Shell ~ 31
Project: Simply Perfect V-Sweater ~ 34
Project: Double Moss Chanel-Style Jacket ~ 38

Chapter 4
Buttonholes ~ 42
Project: Triangle Purse ~ 43
Project: Mock-Rib Cardigan ~ 45

Chapter 5
Color Knitting (Intarsia) ~ 50
Project: Intarsia Purse ~ 52
Project: Asymmetric-Band Jacket ~ 56

Chapter 6
New Stitches ~ 61
Project: No Horizontal Stripes for Me ~ 64
Project: Linen Stitch Shell ~ 68
Project: Poodle Purse and Scarf ~ 72
Project: Diamonds and Cables ~ 74

Chapter 7
Beads in Knitting ~ 79
Project: Looped Beaded Purse ~ 80

Chapter 8
Lace Basics ~ 82
Project: Lace Scarf ~ 84
Project: Beaded Lace Shell ~ 86

Mathematics ~ 90

Glossary of Terms and Abbreviations ~ 94

Resources ~ 95

Introduction

This book is written for those of you who want to learn as much about knitting as possible. Each chapter addresses a new technique and includes patterns to let you practice the skills you've learned. I've chosen techniques and projects to maximize each lesson and reinforce previous lessons.

There are many small projects that are perfect for learning techniques without overwhelming new knitters, and many larger projects for those who are looking for a challenge. As a shop owner, I see the problems knitters have with written patterns and have tried to address those problems by adding detailed explanations and close-up photographs of different parts of each project.

While every knitter is different, so is every designer. My hope as a designer is to connect with those knitters who are looking to learn new things. I believe that if you can continue to gain new skills, whether it be seeing the difference between a knit stitch and a purl stitch or learning how to sew perfect shoulder seams, your love for the craft will never wane.

As a mathematician with a small amount of creativity thrown in, I have tried to compile the best of my work from written patterns and class lectures with information I've learned as a shop owner. Pictures and explanations abound, along with examples within the text. To keep things simple, I've rounded off all measurements to the nearest half inch and have included instructions for metric conversions on page 90. I've also included a "Glossary of Terms and Abbreviations" on page 94.

CHAPTER 1

Knitting Basics

This chapter explains basic knitting techniques. If you're a new knitter, read through this section to familiarize yourself with the techniques. If you're experienced, use this section to look up any technique that is not familiar to you as you are working on a project.

CASTING ON

There are several different ways to cast on. I used the long-tail cast on and the knit cast on for the projects in this book.

Long-Tail Cast On

This is the most common knitting cast on. It creates a stretchy edging that is appropriate for use in almost any project.

Setup: Make a slipknot in the working yarn. Place the slipknot on the right needle and cast on from there.

1. Hold the working yarn over your left index finger, and the tail over your left thumb as shown (fig. 1).

2. Move thumb close to index finger, creating a loop, and insert the needle through the loop on your thumb from bottom to top (fig. 2).

3. Grab the yarn that is around your finger and pull the yarn back down through the loop on your thumb (fig. 3).

4. Release the thumb loop and tighten the new stitch.

Repeat until you have as many stitches as required.

Hint: There should be enough yarn before the slipknot (the "tail") to cast on the required number of stitches. For each stitch to be cast on, leave about one inch of yarn before the slipknot.

Example: You need to cast on 100 stitches. Measure about 100" or about 3 yards (about 3 arm lengths). Make your slipknot here.

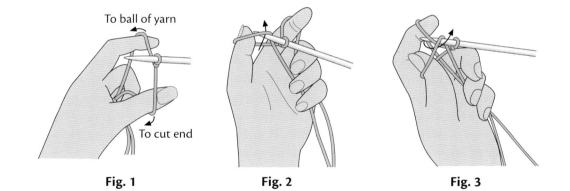

To ball of yarn

To cut end

Fig. 1   **Fig. 2**   **Fig. 3**

Knit Cast On

This cast on is useful for projects with a large number of stitches. There is no "long tail." The cast on is worked with only one strand of yarn. This cast on is also used to cast on stitches at the end of a row.

1. Make a slipknot on the needle, leaving a few inches of yarn to be woven in later.

2. Knit into this stitch, but do not slip it off the left needle.

3. Place the stitch just made onto the left needle, twisting it as shown.

4. There are now two stitches on the left needle and none on the right needle.

5. Knit into the new stitch, but do not slip it off the left needle.

6. Place the stitch just made onto the left needle (one more stitch cast on).

Repeat steps 5 and 6 until the required number of stitches are on the left needle.

NOTE: When casting on at the end of a row, be careful when counting the stitches newly cast on; the first stitch is separated from the rest but still needs to be counted.

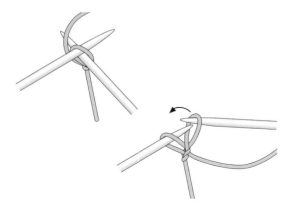

KNIT STITCH

You must hold the working yarn to the back of your work to perform the knit stitch.

1. Insert the right needle from front to back (from right to left) into the first stitch on the left needle (fig. 4).

2. Wrap yarn around the needle in a counterclockwise direction (fig. 5).

3. Draw up the loop on the right needle (fig. 6) and drop the original stitch off the left needle (fig. 7).

Fig. 4

Fig. 5

Fig. 6

Fig. 7

PURL STITCH

You must hold the working yarn to the front of your work to perform the purl stitch.

1. Insert the right needle from back to front (from right to left) into the first stitch on the left needle (fig. 8).

2. Wrap yarn around the needle in a counterclockwise direction (fig. 9).

3. Draw up the loop on the right needle (fig. 10) and drop the original stitch off the left needle (fig. 11).

Fig. 8

Fig. 9

Fig. 10

Fig. 11

CHANGING FROM KNIT TO PURL

Remember that the yarn must be in the correct position before you insert the right needle into the stitch.

- To go from a knit to a purl, bring the yarn from the back of the work to the front of the work between the needles.

- To go from a purl to a knit, bring the yarn from the front of the work to the back of the work between the needles.

- Make sure that you do not bring the yarn over the needle when switching stitches.

JOINING A NEW BALL OF YARN

Do not tie knots to connect the end of an old ball of yarn with the beginning of a new ball. Knots tend to poke through to the outside of your garment. You can tie temporary knots to keep the yarn from getting too loose, but untie them when you finish knitting, before you weave in the ends.

1. When you need to start a new ball of yarn, make sure to leave about 4" of the old ball to weave in later (fig. 12).

2. Overlap the ends (new and old) about 4" and knit or purl one stitch with both yarns (fig. 13).

3. Drop the ends and continue working with the new ball only.

HINT: If the edge will be sewn into a seam on a sweater or other item, try to start a new ball at the end of a row.

If the edge will be visible as on an afghan, a scarf, or a shawl, start a new ball at least a few stitches in from the edge.

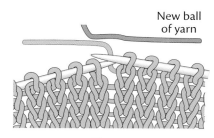

New ball of yarn

Fig. 12

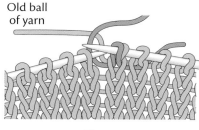

Old ball of yarn

Fig. 13

Knots in Yarn

No matter the quality or price of a yarn, there is always the possibility that you will find a knot as you are knitting. While this is very frustrating, it is a fact of knitting life. When you come to a knot, untie it and treat the ends like a new ball of yarn.

BINDING OFF

Binding off, also called casting off, is the process used to finish a knitted piece or create shaping, such as in an armhole, shoulder, or neck. When stitches are bound off, they are no longer in danger of unraveling. Binding off is only done at the beginning of a row.

When a pattern gives the number of stitches to bind off, the stitch remaining on the right needle is not counted in that number. If the pattern says to bind off all stitches, you will have one stitch on the right needle to fasten off. No stitches will remain on the left needle.

Unless otherwise specified, bind off with a normal tension.

- If your bind off is too tight (the edge looks gathered and has no elasticity), you can use a larger needle to work the bind-off row.

- If your bind off is too loose (the edge looks rippled and floppy), you can use a smaller needle to work the bind-off row.

Binding Off Knitwise

1. Knit the next two stitches; pass the first stitch over the second stitch and off the right needle. One stitch remains on the right needle.

2. Knit one more stitch and pass the remaining stitch over the new one and off the right needle.

Repeat step 2 until you have bound off the correct number of stitches.

Binding Off Purlwise

1. Purl the next two stitches; pass the first stitch over the second stitch and off the right needle. One stitch remains on the right needle.

2. Purl one more stitch and pass the remaining stitch over the new one and off the right needle.

Repeat step 2 until you have bound off the correct number of stitches.

Binding Off in Pattern

1. Work the next two stitches in the stated stitch pattern, pass the first stitch over the second stitch and off the right needle. One stitch remains on the right needle.

2. Work one more stitch in pattern and pass the remaining stitch over the new one and off the right needle.

Repeat step 2 until you have bound off the correct number of stitches.

WEAVING IN ENDS

When you are finished with a garment, there will be ends from new balls of yarn, knots, and so forth. All of these ends must be taken care of to prevent unraveling of stitches and holes in your knitting.

If your ends are long enough and at the edge of the piece, use them for seaming. Otherwise, each end must be secured to prevent holes in your knitting.

Weaving In at Edge

1. Thread the end onto a tapestry needle.

2. Work the needle through about 2" of stitches, straight up the edge of the knitting, and pull the yarn through.

3. Turn your work and weave the end in about 1" in the opposite direction.

4. Cut the end, leaving about ½".

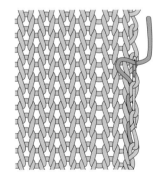

Weaving In in the Middle of Knitting

1. Thread the end onto a tapestry needle.

2. Work the needle through about 2" of stitches on wrong side of work, going across one row of knitting horizontally, and pull the yarn through.

3. Turn your work and weave the end in about 1" in the opposite direction.

4. Cut the end, leaving about ½".

Mistake-Rib Afghan

This easy-to-knit afghan is worked in a sumptuous wool-and-alpaca blend yarn. The "mistake" rib is an easy stitch pattern to master; remember to start every row with two knit stitches and you are ready. The combination of wool and alpaca with a ribbed stitch makes for incredible warmth. This project is perfect for winter; as you knit, the blanket keeps you warm.

Skill Level: Beginner ◼☐☐☐

Finished Size: 48" x 60"

MATERIALS
14 hanks of Ultra Alpaca from Berroco (50% wool, 50% alpaca; 3½ oz, 100 g; 215 yds, 198 m), color 6248 (green) (5)
Size 13 (9 mm) circular needles, at least 24" long, or size required to obtain gauge

GAUGE
12 sts and 20 rows = 4" in mistake rib
NOTE: Gauge is not critical for this project. See chapter 2 for more information.

MISTAKE RIB
(multiple of 4 sts + 1)
All rows: *K2, P2*; rep from * to * to last st, K1.

DIRECTIONS
CO 145 sts.

Work in mistake rib until piece measures 60".

BO all sts.

FINISHING
Weave in all ends.

Spray lightly with water and lay flat to dry.

CHAPTER 2

Gauge, Shaping, and Finishing

After learning the basics of knitting and making a simple project, you're ready to learn the details required to make garments. This chapter will help you gather those skills.

GAUGE

Gauge is a measurement of how many stitches and rows will fit into a certain number of inches or centimeters. Gauge is also called tension; the terms are interchangeable. Gauge is the most important aspect of a knitted garment. If your gauge is not correct, the garment will not be the size you intended it to be. No one wants to make a swatch (a knitted piece to test gauge), but the extra time is well worth it. Never assume that the needle size called for in the pattern is the size you will use. It might be, but it might not. Another reason to check gauge is to give you practice working the stitch pattern. Sometimes after making a gauge swatch, you may decide that you don't like knitting that particular stitch pattern. You have just saved yourself a lot of time and money by discovering this with a small piece rather than an entire garment.

Each pattern will give the gauge used in that particular garment pattern. A specific yarn and specific knitting stitch will also be given. Yarns can be substituted as long as the gauge is the same as the given gauge. When you make a swatch, make sure you use the correct stitch.

For simplicity's sake, when referring to your knitting in this section, I will use only *stitch gauge*. To calculate row gauge, you can use the same procedures (see page 15).

Gauge can be measured in two ways: *stitches per inch* or *overall gauge*.

+ *Stitches per inch* refers to the number of stitches contained in one inch of knitting, measured across the stitches. This type of measurement is usually used to measure gauge on a smooth yarn or simple stitch pattern, such as stockinette stitch or garter stitch.

+ *Overall gauge* is a length measurement for a specific number of stitches. This type of measurement is normally used when measuring gauge over a novelty yarn or more complicated stitch pattern, such as cables or lace.

To check your gauge:

1. Determine the gauge used in the pattern. This should be listed at the beginning of the pattern.

2. Determine the stitch used to obtain this gauge.

3. Cast on as many stitches as the pattern requires to make a swatch at least 4" (10 cm) wide.

NOTE: If your pattern gives gauge over a measurement larger than 4", make your swatch at least that wide.

4. Work in the pattern stitch until the swatch is at least 2" long. The more you knit, the more accurate your swatch will be.

Number of Stitches per Inch

To calculate the number of stitches per inch:

1. Place two pins in your knitting, 1" apart. (Always measure in the middle of your swatch at least 1" down from the needle and 1" above the cast-on edge.)

2. Count the number of stitches between the pins. Make sure you count half stitches.

+ If this number is larger than the required gauge (there are too many stitches contained in one inch), your gauge is too tight and you need to try a larger needle.

• If this number is smaller than the required gauge (there are not enough stitches in one inch), your gauge is too loose and you need to try a smaller needle.

EXAMPLE

Pattern stitch gauge is 3½ sts to 1" in St st.

CO 15 sts.

Work in St st for 2".

Mark the middle 1"; there are 3 stitches between the pins.

You have fewer than 3½ stitches in 1". Your gauge is too loose; you need to try a smaller needle.

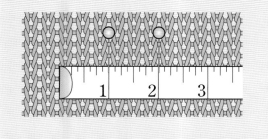

Overall Stitch Gauge

This method is easier to use if the swatch you are checking contains more complicated patterns, such as cables or lace. To compensate for curling edges, it helps to add one stitch that is not worked into the pattern at each end of your swatch.

To calculate overall stitch gauge:

1. Cast on the number of stitches called for in the gauge section of the pattern, plus two extra edge stitches, and knit in pattern for at least 2".

2. Place a pin at each end of your swatch, inside the two edge stitches.

3. Measure the number of inches between the pins. For the best fit, measure as accurately as possible; to the closest ⅛" is preferred.

• If this number is larger than the given gauge (too many inches in your set of stitches), your gauge is too loose and you need to try a smaller needle.

• If this number is smaller than the given gauge (not enough inches in your set of stitches), your gauge is too tight and you need to try a larger needle.

EXAMPLE

Pattern stitch gauge is 12 sts to 4" in St st.

CO 14 sts.

Work in St st for 2".

Place pins at edges of knitting, being careful to unroll edges.

The distance between the pins measures 3½". Your gauge is too tight; you need to try a larger needle.

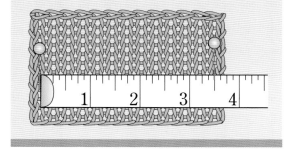

Row Gauge

To calculate row gauge, make a swatch as for measuring the stitch gauge, but count the number of rows instead of the number of stitches. Row gauge is generally not as important as stitch gauge; a pattern will tell you if the row gauge is critical.

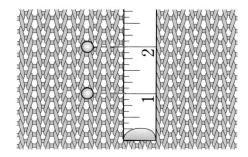

Gauge Facts

For each change in needle size, you can expect a change of about a half a stitch per inch. Do *not* assume that changing needle size will automatically make your gauge correct. You must repeat the swatch with different needles until you find the needle size that works. When you need to change the needle size, don't rip the first swatch; just continue with larger needles. This saves yarn and time and gives you the opportunity to compare the different gauges.

INCREASING

Increasing makes a knitted piece get wider. Each of the following methods for increasing will add one stitch to your total stitch count for the row. When an increase of more than one stitch at a time is required, the pattern will give directions for the specific increase to be used.

Make One (M1)

This method is fairly invisible and can be done both knit- and purlwise. Be careful to follow the instructions closely. If you accidentally put the right needle into the wrong part of the new stitch, there will be a hole in your knitting. The strand between the stitches that you have picked up should look twisted when the increase is done.

NEEDLE CONVERSIONS

Metric sizes are the most accurate way to judge needle size. It doesn't matter where the pattern was written or where the needles were manufactured; metric measurements are unaffected. As you can see in the table below, the same U.S. or English sizes may be assigned to a different metric measurement by different manufacturers, and some metric sizes have no English equivalents.

Metric (mm)	U.S.	English
2	0	14
2.25	1	13
2.5	1	13
2.75	2	12
3	3	11
3.25	3	—
3.5	4	10
3.75	5	9
4	6	—
4.25	6	8
4.5	7	7
5	8	6
5.5	9	5
6	10	4
6.5	10½	3
7	10¾	2
8	11	0
9	13	00
10	15	000
12	17	—
15	19	—
19	35	—
20	36	—
25	50	—

M1 Knitwise

Unless otherwise specified in the pattern, use this method when the increase will be between two knit stitches:

1. Make sure yarn is in back of work.
2. Insert the left needle into the horizontal bar between the last stitch knitted and the next stitch in line to be knitted, from front to back (fig. 14).
3. Insert the right needle into the back of this "stitch." The right needle will be on the back of the knitting (fig. 15). This can be a little tricky; relax and take your time.
4. Knit this "stitch."

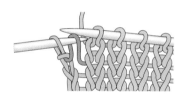

Fig. 14

Fig. 15

M1 Purlwise

Unless otherwise specified in the pattern, use this method when the increase will be between two purl stitches:

1. Make sure yarn is in front of work.
2. Insert the left needle into the horizontal bar between the last stitch knitted and the next stitch in line to be knitted, from back to front.
3. Insert the right needle into the front of this "stitch" in the same manner as for a normal purl.
4. Purl this "stitch."

Knit into Front and Back of Stitch (kfb)

This increase is very easy to make, but it creates a "bump" in the knitted fabric.

1. Knit the next stitch on the left needle, but do not slide it off the left needle yet (fig. 16).
2. Bring the right needle over the stitch just made, and insert it into the back of the same stitch that you have just knit into on the left needle (fig. 17).
3. Knit the stitch again and slide the original stitch off the left needle.

Fig. 16

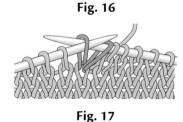

Fig. 17

Purl into Front and Back of Stitch (pfb)

This increase creates a "bump" in the purled fabric.

1. Purl the next stitch on the left needle, but do not slide it off the left needle yet.
2. Bring the right needle over the stitch and insert it into the back of the same stitch that you have just purled on the left needle, from back to front.
3. Purl the stitch again and slide the original stitch off the left needle.

Pick Up Purl Loop on Wrong Side

This method is fairly invisible and works best if used on the purl side of your work.

1. Insert the right needle into the next purl stitch, one row below current row, lifting it away from the knitting.
2. Place this stitch onto the left needle without twisting it (fig. 18).
3. Purl this stitch as you would normally purl (fig. 19). Be careful when slipping this stitch off the left needle after it has been purled so the next stitch does not fall off.

Fig. 18

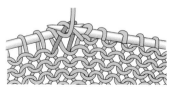

Fig. 19

Backwards Loop

This method is fairly invisible on most knitted fabrics. On extremely bulky knitting, there may be a small hole at the increase.

1. At point of increase, loop the yarn around your finger and slip this loop onto the right needle.

2. On the next row, work this loop into the stitch pattern.

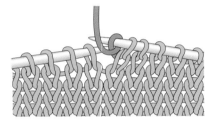

DECREASING

Decreasing makes a knitted piece narrower. Each of the following methods for decreasing will subtract one stitch from your total stitch count for the row. When a decrease of more than one stitch is required, the pattern will give directions for the specific decrease to be used.

Full-fashioned decreasing refers to the placement and direction of decreases on a knitted piece. Decreases normally slant to the left or right and can follow the line of the decreased edge or slant into the middle of the garment. The decreases that slant towards the middle are usually worked a few stitches in from the knitted edge and are considered full-fashioned decreases. Most full-fashioned decreases are worked for decorative as opposed to structural purposes.

Knit Two Together (K2tog)

This creates a decrease that slants to the right. In general, the knit-two-together decrease is used for shaping on the left edge of a knitted piece, so the decrease slants in toward the garment.

1. Insert the right needle into the next two stitches on the left needle at the same time.

2. Knit these two stitches together.

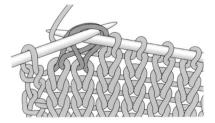

Slip, Slip, Knit (ssk)

This creates a decrease that slants to the left. It is a mirror image of knit two together and is generally used for shaping on the right edge of a knitted piece.

1. Slip the next two stitches, one at a time, from the left needle to the right needle as if to knit.

2. Insert the left needle into the front of these two stitches from left to right (fig. 20).

3. Knit these two stitches together (fig. 21).

4. Slip both stitches off the left needle.

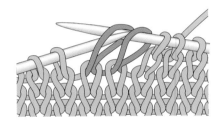

Fig. 20

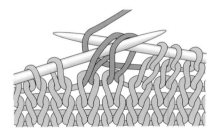

Fig. 21

KNITTING IN THE ROUND

Knitting in the round is a technique used to create seamless tubes. You will see this technique used in this book for neckbands and armhole borders. There are many other uses for knitting in the round, such as making seamless hats and socks. The technique is the same as listed below.

When you are knitting in the round, you never turn your work; you are always working on the right side of the knitting. To join your work, insert the right needle into the first stitch picked up or cast on (instead of the last stitch as in flat knitting).

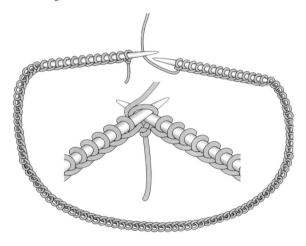

If you put your knitting down and can't remember which direction you were knitting, just make sure that the needle in your right hand is the one that has the yarn coming from it.

POINTERS FOR KNITTING IN THE ROUND

- To work stockinette stitch in the round, knit every row.

- To work garter stitch in the round, alternate knit and purl rounds.

- To bind off, continue in the round (don't turn your work around) and bind off all of the stitches. To create a smooth finished edge, when you have bound off all stitches (there is only one stitch left on the right needle), cut your yarn, leaving a 4" tail. Thread this yarn onto a tapestry needle and sew through the first stitch bound off and then through the last stitch. Pull the tail tight, creating a smooth edge and securing your knitting.

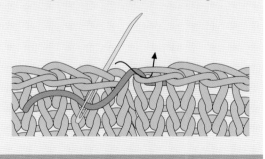

SEWING SEAMS

Three basic types of seams are used to assemble most garments. Variations and combinations of these basic seams can be used to assemble any knitted project.

For most sweater projects, one or both shoulder seams are sewn first, followed by sleeve to body seams, and lastly, side and sleeve seams. Make sure to read the finishing instructions in your specific pattern to determine the order in which seams should be completed.

Practice makes perfect. Allow yourself to make mistakes and learn from them. Keep trying to make your seams look a little more professional each time you assemble a sweater. There is a big difference between homemade and hand knit; finishing procedures are the key.

When seaming, clean off a flat surface so the pieces can be spread out. This makes it much easier to see the edges and seam lines. All seams are sewn from the top of work, with the right sides of both pieces facing up. For all but shoulder seams, a matching smooth yarn may be used if the knitting is done in a novelty yarn with an unusual texture, such as thick-and-thin or bouclé.

Use lots of pins to avoid puckering at the ends of seams. Remember that knitting is not an exact science; be willing to fudge a few stitches or rows if necessary.

If you left long ends when you cast on and bound off your knitting, you can use these tails of knitting yarn for seaming to reduce the number of ends to weave in.

Stitches to Stitches

The stitches-to-stitches seam is most commonly used for sewing shoulder seams.

1. Start at the sleeve edge of the shoulder seam and work toward the neck.

2. To begin the seam, pick up half of the first stitch and half of the next stitch on one shoulder edge, and do the same on the other piece.

3. To continue, go into the next stitch and take two strands (one full stitch) onto the tapestry needle. Repeat on the other piece.

4. Repeat step 3, working from side to side, until the seam is completed.

Repeat the seam on the second shoulder.

When working a seam across shoulders with shaping, you will be picking up one-half of a stitch in one row and one-half of a stitch two rows up. This looks like a giant jump, but it is correct.

For stockinette stitch, do not make the seam stitches too tight. The seam should resemble a row of knitting.

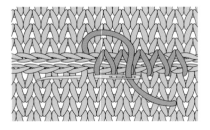

Row to Row

The row-to-row seam is commonly used to sew side and sleeve seams.

1. Begin at the bottom of the seam.

2. Bring the sewing yarn through the very bottom of each edge to ensure even edges (fig. 22).

3. Working the seam one full stitch in from the edge, pick up two "rungs" on each side (fig. 23).

HINT: If you have trouble finding the "ladder" along a knitted edge, use a contrast-color yarn and baste along the stitch two stitches in from the edge on each piece.

Repeat step 3 until the seam is finished.

Fig. 22

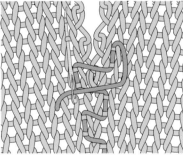

Fig. 23

Stitches to Row

The stitches-to-row seam is most commonly used to sew sleeves onto a sweater body. It combines both of the previous techniques.

1. Fold the sleeve in half and mark the middle with a pin; attach the center of the sleeve to the shoulder seam with a pin.

2. With right sides facing up, begin sewing at shoulder seam. Use a long piece of yarn, but only pull through half of it for the first stitch.

3. Working from shoulder to underarm on one side:

   + On sleeve (stitches), pick up two strands (one entire stitch).

   + On body (rows), pick up one or two "rungs" for each stitch.

4. Repeat step 3 until seam is sewn to underarm, easing the sleeve evenly throughout if necessary.

5. Go back to the shoulder seam and pick up the remainder of the sewing yarn; sew in the opposite direction to underarm, easing as necessary. If you are more comfortable sewing in one direction, turn your entire garment around to go in the "right" direction.

Hints for Successful Seaming while Knitting

There are many things that can be done in the course of knitting a garment that will make it easier to finish the garment. If you can incorporate at least one of the following procedures in your knitting, you will find that seaming is much less difficult.

- On sleeves or side edges, work increases and decreases one or two stitches in from the edge. This will give you a clean selvage edge to sew up.

- When decreases must be at the edge of a piece for set-in sleeve caps and some raglan shaping, make decreases that follow the line of the edge. Use ssk at beginning of row, and K2tog at end of row.

- When binding off in groups (shoulder and neck shaping), slip (don't knit or purl) the first stitch of each row on successive bind offs.

- When binding off in groups (when edge will be seamed), always bind off in stockinette stitch (knit on right side, purl on wrong side).

BLOCKING

Blocking is a very broad term that refers to the finishing after all of the knitting and sewing are done. Most projects can be blocked very simply with a steam iron. Separate pieces of a garment may be blocked or an entire garment can be blocked after it is sewn together.

For lace and cables, it is easier to get the right shape and dimensions if pieces are blocked before sewing. Each piece is laid out on a flat surface (a spare mattress, blocking board, or carpet will all work) and pinned to the correct measurements. Spray the pieces with water and leave pinned until dry.

For flat knitting (color work, stockinette stitch), the pieces can be sewn together and then blocked with a steam iron. Set the iron to the hottest setting and use a wet cloth between the iron and your knitting. Iron as you would a fabric shirt, but just press the iron down—do not slide it around.

Remember that a plain stockinette-stitch piece will curl at the edges. Blocking will help but not eliminate this effect. If the edge is sewn into a seam, the curling will cease at the seam. If the edge is free (bottom edge or neckline), it will curl even if it seems to lay flat after ironing.

Basic V-neck Cardigan

Two strands of yarn combine to create this very simple, yet practical cardigan. Try using a novelty yarn and a basic yarn or even two novelties for a completely different look. The modified set-in sleeve eliminates a lot of the bulk of a drop-shoulder sweater, but is easy to knit and assemble.

Skill Level: Easy ■■□□

Finished Bust: 41 (43, 45, 47, 49, 51)" when buttoned
Finished Length: 22 (22, 23, 23, 24, 24)"

MATERIALS

7 (7, 7, 8, 8, 9) hanks of Summer Tweed from Rowan (70% silk, 30% cotton; 50 g; 118 yds, 108 m), color 540 (red) (4)

7 (7, 8, 8, 9, 9) balls of All Seasons Cotton from Rowan (60% cotton, 40% acrylic; 50 g; 98 yds, 90 m), color 223 (red) (4)

Size 13 (9 mm) needles or size required to obtain gauge

Size 11 (8 mm) needles

5 markers for buttonhole placement

5 buttons, 1½" to 2"

Sewing needle and matching thread

GAUGE

10 sts and 16 rows = 4" in St st using larger needles and both yarns held tog

BACK

With smaller needles and both yarns held tog, CO 50 (53, 55, 58, 60, 63) sts.

Knit 4 rows.

Change to larger needles and St st.

Work even until piece measures 14", ending with WS row.

Cut-in armhole eliminates bulk under the arm.

Back neck border is created as back is knit.

Shape Armhole

BO 5 sts at beg of next 2 rows—40 (43, 45, 48, 50, 53) sts.

Work even until armhole measures 7, (7, 8, 8, 9, 9)", ending with RS row.

Back Neck Border

Next row (WS): P6 (8, 8, 9, 9, 10), K28 (27, 29, 30, 32, 33), P6 (8, 8, 9, 9, 10).

Next row (RS): Knit.

Rep last 2 rows once more and then first row again.

BO all sts loosely.

LEFT FRONT

With smaller needles and both yarns held tog, CO 30 (31, 33, 34, 35, 36) sts.

Knit 4 rows.

Change to larger needles and cont as follows:

    Row 1 (RS): Knit.

    Row 2 (WS): K5, purl to end of row.

Rep rows 1 and 2 until piece measures 14", ending with WS row.

Shape Armhole

Next row (RS): BO 5 sts at beg of row—25 (26, 28, 29, 30, 31) sts rem.

Shape V-neck

Next row (WS): K5, purl to end of row.

Next row: Knit to last 7 sts, K2tog, K5.

Rep last 2 rows until 11 (13, 13, 14, 14, 15) sts rem.

Work even until piece measures same as back.

BO all sts.

Mark position for 5 buttons, the first ¾" from bottom edge and the last at the beginning of the V-neck shaping, with the rest equally spaced between these.

RIGHT FRONT

With smaller needles and both yarns held tog, CO 30 (31, 33, 34, 35, 36) sts.

Knit 4 rows.

Change to larger needles and cont as follows:

    Next row (RS) (buttonhole): K3, YO, K2tog, knit to end of row.

    Next row (WS): Purl to last 5 sts, K5.

Cont as follows:

    Row 1 (RS): Knit.

    Row 2 (WS): Purl to last 5 sts, K5.

Rep rows 1 and 2 until piece measures 14", ending with RS row. AT THE SAME TIME, make buttonholes to correspond to markers on left front.

Shape Armhole

Next row (WS): BO 5 sts at beg of row—25 (26, 28, 29, 30, 31) sts rem.

Shape V-neck

Next row (RS): K5, ssk, knit to end.

Next row: Purl to last 5 sts, K5.

Rep last 2 rows until 11 (13, 13, 14, 14, 15) sts rem.

Work even until piece measures same as back. BO all sts.

SLEEVES (make 2)

With smaller needles and both yarns held tog, CO 22 (22, 24, 24, 26, 26) sts.

Knit 4 rows.

Change to larger needles and cont in St st.

Inc 1 st at each end of every 6th row 9 (9, 10, 10, 12, 12) times—40 (40, 44, 44, 50, 50) sts.

Work even until sleeve measures 20".

BO all sts loosely.

FINISHING

Sew shoulder seams.

Sew armhole edge of sleeve to straight edge of armhole, and sew top 2" of sleeve to bound-off edges at armhole.

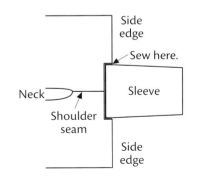

Sew sleeve seams and side seams.

Sew on buttons to correspond with buttonholes.

Steam seams lightly if desired.

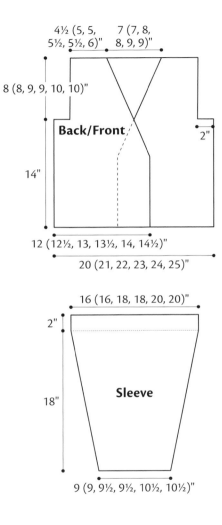

CHAPTER 3

Edgings and Bands

To add a neckband and button bands to a sweater or an armhole edging to a vest, you can pick up stitches around the opening, then knit the borders. You can also use crochet to add edgings to garments. Both types of edgings are covered in this chapter, to give you different techniques to add to your skill set.

PICKING UP STITCHES

Always pick up stitches with the right side of the project facing you, unless specifically stated otherwise in the pattern.

1. Insert the needle from the right side to the wrong side, all the way through the knitting.

2. Wrap the yarn around the needle and pull up a stitch.

HINT: If the knitting you are picking up from is too tight to insert a knitting needle, use a crochet hook to pull up stitches and then transfer them to the knitting needle.

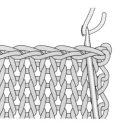 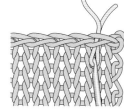

Insert crochet hook. Draw up loop.

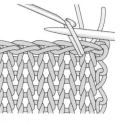

Place loop on needle.

Pick up stitches from right to left with the knitting facing you.

Front Bands

Pick up stitches one full stitch in from edge. Along a straight edge, pick up 1" of stitches for every inch of rows.

EXAMPLE

Your actual knitted gauge is 6½ rows and 5 stitches per inch.

For each 6½ rows, pick up 5 stitches along edge.

Or (more reasonably), pick up 10 stitches for every 13 rows (2").

If you are within five or six stitches of what the pattern calls for, make your bands. If you are way off on the stitch count, go back and pick up more or fewer stitches. Some patterns have a specific reason for an unusual number of stitches.

Neckbands

Beginning at left shoulder unless otherwise indicated in pattern, pick up stitches along left front neck edge. If there is a straight portion (no shaping), pick up stitches as for button band. Along neck shaping, pick up stitches as they were bound off.

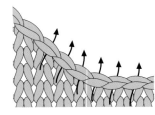

Stitches picked up on curved edge with decreases

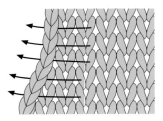

Stitches picked up on V-neck with decreases

EXAMPLE

When knitting neck shaping on the front of a sweater, the pattern calls for binding off 4 stitches, 3 stitches, 2 stitches, and then 1 stitch every other row 4 times (total of 13 stitches).

To pick up stitches smoothly along this edge, pick up 1 stitch in each bound-off stitch for a total of 13.

When there is a gap between stitches on a garment, do not pick up a stitch there; skip over the gap and pick up the next stitch.

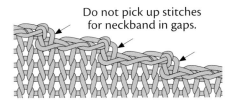

Do not pick up stitches for neckband in gaps.

Along the center-front straight portion of the neck, pick up one stitch in each bound-off stitch. Work up the shaped portion of the right side of the neck in the same manner as for the left. Pick up along the back neck in the same manner as for the center-front neck.

If you are within five or six stitches of what the pattern calls for, knit your neckband. If you are way off on the stitch count, go back and pick up more or fewer stitches. Some patterns have a specific reason for an unusual number of stitches.

CROCHET

In this book, we will discuss crochet as a finishing agent. The following instructions assume that you hold the hook in your right hand. It is easier to hold the yarn in your left hand, but it is not necessary. If you have never crocheted before, you may want to make a knitted swatch and practice making crocheted borders on that.

When you are ready to crochet a border on a finished garment, work the edge for about 4" and then check to make sure your tension is correct. The garment edge should lie flat. If your tension is too tight, the edge will gather. If your tension is too loose, the edge will ripple.

Chain Stitch

Chain stitch in crochet is analogous to casting on in knitting. It creates a foundation for working other stitches. Chain stitch is also used to make long strings for ties and to create picots and button loops.

1. Make a slipknot and place it on the hook.
2. Wrap the yarn around the hook and draw the yarn through.

Repeat step 2 until the chain has the required number of stitches.

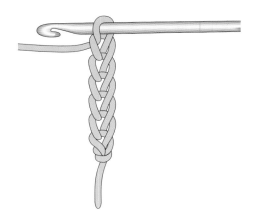

Joining Crochet to a Knitted Piece

Insert the crochet hook into a stitch on the edge of the knitting and draw a loop through to the front. Wrap the yarn around the hook and draw a second loop through the first to secure.

Slip Stitch (sl st)

Slip stitches are worked from right to left over the edge of a knitted piece. The stitch works up quickly and creates a smooth edge without adding any height.

1. With the right side of the knitted piece facing you, insert the hook into a knitted stitch (fig. 24).
2. Wrap the yarn around the hook (fig. 25) and draw the yarn through both the stitch and the loop on the hook; one loop remains on hook (fig. 26).

Repeat steps 1 and 2 across the piece for a slip-stitch edge.

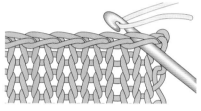

Fig. 24

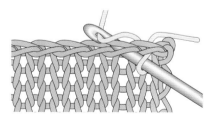

Fig. 25

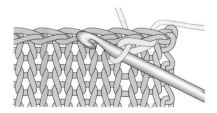

Fig. 26

Single Crochet (sc)

Single-crochet stitches are worked from right to left over the edge of a knitted piece. Single crochet creates a smooth edge and adds a little height.

1. With the right side of the knitted piece facing you, insert the hook into a knitted stitch.
2. Wrap the yarn around the hook and draw up a loop; two loops on hook.
3. Wrap the yarn around the hook and draw the yarn through both loops (fig. 27); one loop remains on hook (fig. 28).

Repeat steps 1–3 across the piece from right to left for a single-crochet edge (fig. 28).

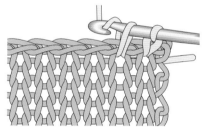

Fig. 27

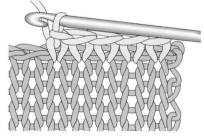

Fig. 28

Crab Stitch (backward single crochet)

Crab stitch is worked from *left to right* over the knitted piece. This stitch is usually worked over a base row of single crochet or slip stitch to create a decorative edge.

Setup: With the right side of the knitted piece facing you, insert the hook into a knitted stitch or a single-crochet stitch and work a single crochet.

1. Insert the hook into the next stitch to the *right* of the stitch just completed.
2. Wrap the yarn around the hook and draw up a loop (fig. 29); two loops are on hook.
3. Wrap the yarn around the hook and draw the yarn through both loops (fig. 30); one loop remains on hook.

Repeat steps 1–3 across the piece from left to right for a crab-stitch edge.

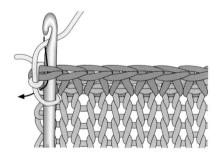

Fig. 29

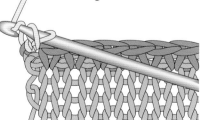

Fig. 30

Evening Jacket

This elegant little number will go anywhere, from Sunday brunch to an evening on the town. The lightweight mohair with random slubs of glitz makes this sweater a superb addition to any wardrobe. You may find that wood or plastic needles are easier to use than metal with this yarn.

Skill Level: Easy ◼◼☐☐

Finished Bust: 38 (40, 42, 44)"
Finished Length: 22 (22, 23, 23)"

MATERIALS

5 (5, 6, 6) balls of Gossamer from Karabella (30% kid mohair, 52% nylon, 18% polyester; 1¾ oz, 50 g; 222 yds, 200 m), color 6105 (green) 🧶**4**

Size 7 (4.5 mm) needles or size required to obtain gauge

Size 5 (3.75 mm) needles

Size F-5 (3.75 mm) crochet hook

GAUGE

20 sts and 26 rows = 4" in St st using larger needles

K1, P1 RIB

(worked over even number of sts)
Row 1: *K1, P1*; rep from * to * to end of row.
Row 2: *P1, K1*; rep from * to * to end of row.
(worked over odd number of sts)
Row 1: *K1, P1*; rep from * to * to last st, K1.
Row 2: *P1, K1*; rep from * to * to last st, P1.

BACK

Using smaller needles, CO 95 (100, 105, 110) sts and work in K1, P1 rib for ¾". Change to larger needles and continue in St st until piece measures 14" (all sizes).

Shape Armhole

BO 4 sts at beg of next 2 rows.

BO 2 sts at beg of next 4 rows.

BO 1 st at beg of next 8 rows—71 (76, 81, 86) sts.

Work even until armhole measures 8 (8, 9, 9)".

Shape Shoulders

BO 6 (6, 6, 6) sts at beg of next 2 rows.

BO 6 (7, 8, 9) sts at beg of next 4 rows.

BO rem 35 (36, 37, 38) sts.

RIGHT FRONT

Using smaller needles, CO 48 (51, 53, 56) sts and work in K1, P1 rib for ¾". Change to larger needles and work in St st until piece measures same as back to armhole, ending with RS row.

Shape Armhole

Next row (WS): BO 4 sts at beg of row.

Work 1 row even.

BO 2 sts at beg of next row.

Work 1 row even.

Rep last 2 rows once more.

BO 1 st at beg of next row.

Work 1 row even.

Rep last 2 rows 3 more times—36 (39, 41, 44) sts.

Cont without shaping until armhole measures 5 (5, 6, 6)", ending with WS row.

Shape Neck

Next row (RS): BO 8 sts at beg of row.

Work 1 row even.

BO 3 sts at beg of next row.

Work 1 row even.

BO 2 sts at beg of next row.

Work 1 row even.

Rep last 2 rows once more.

BO 1 st at beg of next row.

Work 1 row even.

Rep last 2 rows 2 (3, 3, 4) more times—18 (20, 22, 24) sts rem.

Work even until piece measures same as back to shoulder shaping, ending with RS row.

Shape Shoulder

Next row (WS): BO 6 (6, 6, 6) sts at beg of row.

Work 1 row even.

BO 6 (7, 8, 9) sts at beg of next row.

Work 1 row even.

BO rem 6 (7, 8, 9) sts.

LEFT FRONT

Work same as right front to armhole, ending with WS row.

Shape Armhole

Next row (RS): BO 4 sts at beg of row.

Work 1 row even.

BO 2 sts at beg of next row.

Work 1 row even.

Rep last 2 rows once more.

BO 1 st at beg of next row.

Work 1 row even.

Rep last 2 rows 3 more times—36 (39, 41, 44) sts.

Cont without shaping until armhole measures 5 (5, 6, 6)", ending with RS row.

Shape Neck

Next row (WS): BO 8 sts at beg of row.

Work 1 row even.

BO 3 sts at beg of next row.

Work 1 row even.

BO 2 sts at beg of next row.

Work 1 row even.

Rep last 2 rows once more.

BO 1 st at beg of next row.

Work 1 row even.

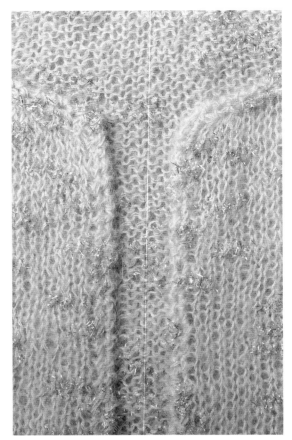

Here's a close-up look at the crocheted borders.

Rep last 2 rows 2 (3, 3, 4) more times—18 (20, 22, 24) sts rem.

Work even until piece measures same as back to shoulder shaping, ending with WS row.

Shape Shoulder
Next row (RS): BO 6 (6, 6, 6) sts at beg of row.

Work 1 row even.

BO 6 (7, 8, 9) sts at beg of next row.

Work 1 row even.

BO rem 6 (7, 8, 9) sts.

SLEEVES (make 2)
With smaller needles, CO 48 sts and work in K1, P1 rib for ¾". Change to larger needles and St st. Inc 1 st at each end of 5th and foll 6th rows 15 (15, 20, 20) times—80 (80, 90, 90) sts.

Work even until piece measures 17 (17, 18, 18)".

Shape Sleeve Cap
BO 4 sts at beg of next 2 rows.

BO 2 sts at beg of next 28 rows.

BO rem 16 (16, 26, 26) sts.

FINISHING
Sew shoulder seams.

Set in sleeves.

Sew side and sleeve seams.

With WS facing, beg at lower left front opening, work 1 row of sc up left front, around neck, and down right front.

Without turning work, work 1 row of crab st over sc row.

Fasten off. Spray lightly with water and lay flat to dry.

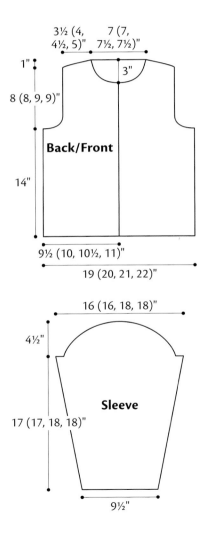

Sideways Summer Shell

Knit from side to side, this tank top makes the most of a self-striping yarn. Simple square shaping adds to the ease of knitting and the stylish look. When picking up stitches for the borders, don't pick up stitches in the corners; borders will round slightly when bound off. The bottom edge is left unfinished; it will roll slightly to the inside for a smooth finish.

Skill Level: Intermediate ◖■■□

Finished Bust: 36 (38, 41, 44, 46)"
Finished Length (all sizes): 23"

MATERIALS
6 (6, 7, 7, 8) balls of Bella Colour from Plymouth Yarn (55% cotton, 45% acrylic; 50 g; 104 yds), color 201 (multicolor) ④

Size 10 (6 mm) needles or size required to obtain gauge

Size 9 (5.5 mm) circular needle, 24" long

1 stitch marker

GAUGE
16 sts and 20 rows to 4" in St st using larger needles

BACK AND FRONT (both alike)

CO 60 (60, 60, 58, 58) sts.

Shape Armhole

Working in St st throughout, inc 1 st at beg of every knit (RS) row 7 (7, 8, 8, 9) times—67 (67, 68, 66, 67) sts. End with RS row.

Next row (WS): CO 25 (25, 24, 26, 25) sts at end of row—92 sts (all sizes).

Work even for 3 (3, 3, 3½, 3½)", ending with WS row. Piece should measure about 6 (6, 6, 6½, 7)".

Shape Neck

Next row (RS): BO 16 sts at beg of row—76 sts (all sizes).

Work even until piece measures 12 (13, 14½, 15½, 17)", ending with RS row.

Next row (WS): CO 16 sts at end of row—92 sts (all sizes).

Work even for 3 (3, 3, 3½, 3½)", ending with WS row. Piece should measure about 15 (16, 17½, 19, 20½)".

Shape Armhole

Next row (RS): BO 25 (25, 24, 26, 25) sts at beg of row—67 (67, 68, 66, 67) sts.

Purl 1 row.

Dec 1 st at beg of every knit (RS) row 7 (7, 8, 8, 9) times—60 (60, 60, 58, 58) sts.

Purl 1 row.

BO all sts loosely.

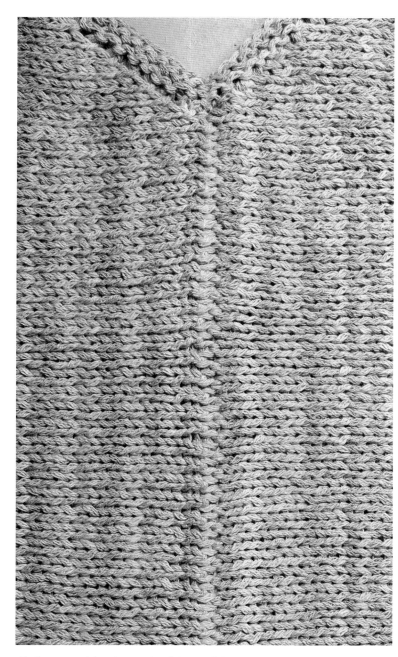

Side seams blend into the fabric of the sweater.

FINISHING

Sew shoulder seams.

Neckband

With RS facing you, smaller needles, and beg at left shoulder seam, PU 16 sts down left front neck, 24 (28, 34, 36, 40) sts across front neck, 16 sts up right front neck, 16 sts down right back neck, 24 (28, 34, 36, 40) sts across back neck, and 16 sts up left back neck—112 (120, 132, 136, 144) sts.

PM and join in a round.

Purl 1 round, knit 1 round, purl 1 round.

BO all sts knitwise.

Armhole Edges (both sides)

With RS facing you, smaller needles, and beg at underarm seam, PU 10 (11, 12, 13, 14) sts along front armhole shaping, 25 (25, 25, 27, 27) sts to shoulder seam, 25 (25, 25, 27, 27) sts to back armhole shaping, 10 (11, 12, 13, 14) sts along back armhole shaping—70 (72, 74, 80, 82) sts.

Knit 3 rows.

BO all sts knitwise.

Sew side seams.

Sew armhole bands together at underarm.

Steam seams lightly if desired.

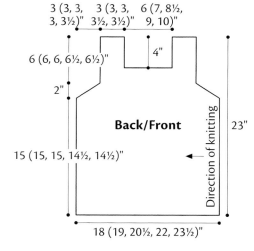

3 (3, 3, 3, 3½)"   3 (3, 3, 3½, 3½)"   6 (7, 8½, 9, 10)"

6 (6, 6, 6½, 6½)"

4"

2"

Back/Front

Direction of knitting

23"

15 (15, 15, 14½, 14½)"

18 (19, 20½, 22, 23½)"

Simply Perfect V-Sweater

For this sweater, I set out to copy the shape of one of my favorite shirts. I knit the decreases a few stitches in from the edge to accentuate the raglan and V-neck shaping. The long ribbings make for a more fitted sweater. If you would like a little less "fitting," make the ribbings shorter and make up the length by knitting the stockinette-stitch portions longer. If you are adding length to either the sleeves or body, make sure to do so before you begin the raglan shaping.

Skill Level: Intermediate ◖■■▭

Finished Bust: 38 (40, 42, 44, 46, 48)"
Finished Length: 22 (22, 23, 23, 24, 24)"

MATERIALS
6 (6, 7, 7, 8, 8) hanks of Clip from On Line (100% cotton; 100 g, 181 yds), color 124 (blue) (4)

Size 7 (4.5 mm) needles or size required to obtain gauge

Size 6 (4 mm) circular needles, 24" long

Stitch holder

Stitch markers

Safety pin

GAUGE
20 sts and 26 rows = 4" in St st using larger needles

SPECIAL STITCHES

K3tog: Knit 3 stitches together (decrease 2 stitches).

sssk: Slip the next 3 stitches as if to knit, one at a time, to right needle. Insert left needle into front of these 3 stitches and knit them together (decrease 2 stitches).

S2KP: Slip next 2 stitches as if to knit 2 together, knit next stitch, and pass 2 slipped stitches over knit stitch.

K1,P1 RIB

(worked over odd number of sts)

Row 1: *K1, P1*; rep from * to * to last st, K1.

Row 2: *P1, K1*; rep from * to * to last st, P1.

Rep rows 1 and 2 for patt.

BACK

With larger needles, CO 95 (101, 105, 111, 115, 121) sts.

Work in K1, P1 rib for 4".

Change to St st. Work even until piece measures 14 (14, 14½, 14½, 15, 15)", ending with WS row.

Shape Raglan Armholes

BO 5 (6, 5, 6, 5, 8) sts at beg of next 2 rows—85 (89, 95, 99, 105, 105) sts.

Next row (RS): K2, K2tog, knit to last 4 sts, ssk, K2.

Next row: Purl.

Rep last 2 rows 21 (21, 23, 23, 25, 25) more times.

BO rem 41 (45, 47, 51, 53, 53) sts.

FRONT

Work same as back to armhole.

Shape Raglan Armholes

BO 5 (6, 5, 6, 5, 8) sts at beg of next 2 rows—85 (89, 95, 99, 105, 105) sts.

Next row (RS): K2, K2tog, knit to last 4 sts, ssk, K2.

Next row (WS): Purl.

Rep last 2 rows 3 more times (all sizes)—77 (81, 87, 91, 97, 97) sts.

Shape V-neck

NOTE: Read pattern carefully; there are ssk and sssk decreases in the neck shaping.

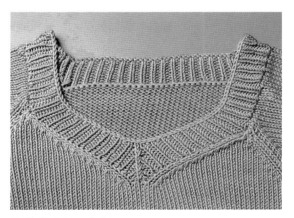

Full-fashioned decreases create an interesting detail.

Left Neck

Next row (RS): K2, K2tog, K29 (31, 34, 36, 39, 39), sssk, K2, place next st on safety pin and rem sts on holder, turn—35 (37, 40, 42, 45, 45) sts for left shoulder.

Next row (WS): Purl.

Next row: K2, K2tog, knit to last 4 sts, ssk, K2.

Next row: Purl.

Next row: K2, K2tog, knit to last 5 sts, sssk, K2.

Rep last 4 rows 6 (6, 7, 7, 8, 8) more times.

For sizes 40" and 44" *only*:
    Next row (WS): Purl.
    Next row: K2, K2tog, knit to last 4 sts, ssk, K2.

Fasten off last st.

Place sts from holder back onto working needle.

Right Neck

Reattach yarn to sts on holder with RS facing you, leaving center st on safety pin. K2, K3tog, K29 (31, 34, 36, 39, 39), ssk, K2—35 (37, 40, 42, 45, 45) sts for right shoulder.

Next row (WS): Purl.

Next row: K2, K2tog, knit to last 4 sts, ssk, K2.

Next row: Purl.

Next row: K2, K3tog, knit to last 5 sts, sssk, K2.

Rep last 4 rows 6 (6, 7, 7, 8, 8) more times.

For sizes 40" and 44" *only*:
    Next row (WS): Purl.
    Next row: K2, K2tog, knit to last 4 sts, ssk, K2.

Fasten off last st.

LEFT SLEEVE

With larger needles, CO 51 (51, 53, 53, 55, 55) sts.

Work in K1, P1 rib for 4", inc 1 st at each end on 11th and foll 6th rows twice—57 (57, 59, 59, 61, 61) sts.

Change to St st and inc 1 st at each end of next and every foll 6th row 6 (6, 7, 7, 9, 9) times—71 (71, 75, 75, 81, 81) sts.

Work even until sleeve measures 13" or desired length to underarm. End with WS row.

Shape Raglan

BO 5 sts at beg of next 2 rows—61 (61, 65, 65, 71, 71) sts.

Next row (RS): K2, K2tog, knit to last 4 sts, ssk, K2.

Next row (WS): Purl.

Next row: Knit.

Next row: Purl.

Rep last 4 rows 3 more times—53 (53, 57, 57, 63, 63) sts.

Next row (RS): K2, K2tog, knit to last 4 sts, ssk, K2.

Next row (WS): Purl.

Rep last 2 rows 10 (10, 12, 12, 14, 14) more times—31 (31, 31, 31, 33, 33) sts. End with WS row.

Shape Neck

NOTE: Top portion of sleeve is part of neck.

Next row (RS): K2, K2tog, knit to end.

Next row: BO 10 sts, purl to end.

Next row: K2, K2tog, knit to end.

Next row: BO 9 (9, 9, 9, 10, 10) sts, purl to end.

Next row: K2, K2tog, knit to end.

Next row: BO rem 9 (9, 9, 9, 10, 10) sts.

RIGHT SLEEVE

Work as for left sleeve to neck shaping.

Shape Neck

Next row (RS): Knit to last 4 sts, ssk, K2.

Next row: Purl.

Next row: BO 10 sts, knit to last 4 sts, ssk, K2.

Next row: Purl.

Next row: BO 9 (9, 9, 9, 10, 10) sts, knit to last 4 sts, ssk, K2.

Next row: Purl.

Next row: BO rem 9 (9, 9, 9, 10, 10) sts.

FINISHING

Sew raglan seams.

Sew side and sleeve seams.

Neckband: With RS facing you, circular needles, and beg at right back raglan seam, PU 38 (44, 46, 50, 52, 56) sts across back, 26 sts across left sleeve, 22 (22, 24, 24, 26, 26) sts down left front neck, PU st from safety pin and mark this st, PU 22 (22, 24, 24, 26, 26) sts up right front neck, and 26 sts across right sleeve, PM to indicate end of round—135 (141, 147, 151, 157, 161) sts. Join in a round.

Rnd 1: *K1, P1*; rep from * to * to 1 st before marked st, S2KP, *P1, K1*; rep from * to * to end of round.

Rnd 2: Work in est rib.

Rep last 2 rows 4 more times. BO all sts knitwise.

Steam seams lightly if desired.

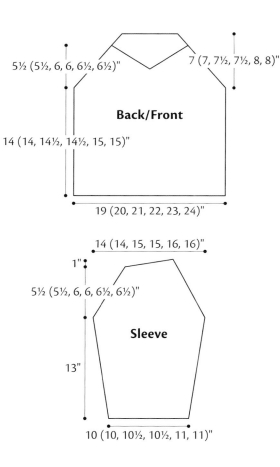

5½ (5½, 6, 6, 6½, 6½)"   7 (7, 7½, 7½, 8, 8)"

Back/Front

14 (14, 14½, 14½, 15, 15)"

19 (20, 21, 22, 23, 24)"

14 (14, 15, 15, 16, 16)"

1"

5½ (5½, 6, 6, 6½, 6½)"

Sleeve

13"

10 (10, 10½, 10½, 11, 11)"

Double Moss Chanel-Style Jacket

I love the double moss stitch in hand-dyed yarns. The combination of knits and purls tends to spread out the colors and give a more even tone to the yarns. You may find that this stitch slants slightly to one side (twists on the bias). This is due to the slightly different tensions we all have between knitting and purling. A damp blocking will cure this annoyance. Since the double moss stitch does not curl, bottom borders are not necessary. I have used a border at the front center to give the jacket a little more structural stability. This border is knit into the fronts as you are working them.

Skill Level: Easy ◼◼☐☐

Finished Bust: 38 (40, 42, 44)" when closed
Finished Length (all sizes): 18"

MATERIALS

4 (4, 5, 5) skeins of Twizzle from Mountain Colors (85% merino wool, 15% silk; 100 g, 250 yds), color Juniper (④)

Size 8 (5 mm) needles or size required to obtain gauge

Size 7 (4.5 mm) needles

1 hook and eye

Sewing needle and matching thread

GAUGE

19 sts and 24 rows = 4" in double moss st using larger needles

DOUBLE MOSS STITCH

(worked over odd number of sts)

Row 1 (RS): *K1, P1*; rep from * to * to last st, K1.

Row 2 (WS): *P1, K1*; rep from * to * to last st, P1.

Row 3: *P1, K1*; rep from * to * to last st, P1.

Row 4: *K1, P1*; rep from * to * to last st, K1.

Rep rows 1–4 for patt.

NOTE: When using hand-dyed yarns, it is advisable to work with two balls of yarn at once. Alternate balls every 2 or 4 rows to prevent color pooling.

BACK
Using smaller needles, CO 91 (97, 101, 105) sts and work in double moss st for 1½".

Change to larger needles and continue in double moss st until piece measures 10" (all sizes).

Shape Armhole
BO 4 sts at beg of next 2 rows.

BO 2 sts at beg of next 4 rows.

BO 1 st at beg of next 8 rows—67 (73, 77, 81) sts.

Work even until armhole measures 8" (all sizes).

Shape Shoulders
BO 5 (5, 5, 7) sts at beg of next 2 rows.

BO 6 (7, 7, 7) sts at beg of next 4 rows.

BO rem 33 (35, 39, 39) sts.

LEFT FRONT
Using smaller needles, CO 49 (51, 55, 57) sts and set up patts as follows:

Row 1 (RS): Work row 1 of double moss st to last 4 sts, sl 1, K1, sl 1, K1.

Row 2 (WS): Sl 1, P1, sl 1, P1, work row 2 of double moss st to end of row.

Row 3: Work row 3 of double moss st to last 4 sts, sl 1, K1, sl 1, K1.

Row 4: Sl 1, P1, sl 1, P1, work row 4 of double moss st to end of row.

Front bands are knit right into the front pieces.

Rep rows 1–4 until piece measures 1½".

Change to larger needles and continue as above (4 sts for front border, remainder of sts in double moss st) until piece measures 10" (all sizes), ending with WS row.

Shape Armhole
Next row (RS): BO 4 sts at beg of row.

Work 1 row even.

BO 2 sts at beg of next row.

Work 1 row even.

Rep last 2 rows once.

BO 1 st at beg of next row.

Work 1 row even.

Rep last 2 rows 3 more times—37 (39, 43, 45) sts.

Cont without shaping until armhole measures 7" (all sizes), ending with RS row.

Shape Neck
Next row (WS): BO 12 sts at beg of row (all sizes).

Work 1 row even.

BO 3 sts at beg of next row (all sizes).

Work 1 row even.

BO 2 sts at beg of next row (all sizes).

Work 1 row even.

For sizes 42" and 44" *only*:
Rep last 2 rows twice more.

All sizes:
BO 1 st at beg of next row.

Work 1 row even.

Rep last 2 rows twice more—17 (19, 19, 21) sts.

Work even until piece measures same as back to shoulder shaping, ending with WS row.

Shape Shoulder
Next row (RS): BO 5 (5, 5, 7) sts at beg of row.

Work 1 row even.

BO 6 (7, 7, 7) sts at beg of next row.

Work 1 row even.

BO rem 6 (7, 7, 7) sts.

RIGHT FRONT

Using smaller needles, CO 49 (51, 55, 57) sts and set up patt as follows:

Row 1 (RS): Sl 1, K1, sl 1, K1, work row 1 of double moss st to end of row.

Row 2 (WS): Work row 2 of double moss st to last 4 sts, sl 1, P1, sl 1, P1.

Row 3: Sl 1, K1, sl 1, K1, work row 3 of double moss st to end of row.

Row 4: Work row 4 of double moss st to last 4 sts, sl 1, P1, sl 1, P1.

Rep rows 1–4 until piece measures 1½".

Change to larger needles and cont as above (4 sts for front border, rem sts in double moss st) until piece measures 10" (all sizes), ending with RS row.

Shape Armhole

Next row (WS): BO 4 sts at beg of row.

Work 1 row even.

BO 2 sts at beg of next row.

Work 1 row even.

Rep last 2 rows once.

BO 1 st at beg of next row.

Work 1 row even.

Rep last 2 rows 3 more times—37 (39, 43, 45) sts.

Cont without shaping until armhole measures 7", ending with WS row.

A hook and eye keeps the jacket fronts in place.

Shape Neck

Next row (RS): BO 12 sts at beg of row (all sizes).

Work 1 row even.

BO 3 sts at beg of next row (all sizes).

Work 1 row even.

BO 2 sts at beg of next row (all sizes).

Work 1 row even.

For sizes 42" and 44" *only*:
 Rep last 2 rows twice more.

All sizes:
 BO 1 st at beg of next row.

 Work 1 row even.

 Rep last 2 rows twice more—17 (19, 19, 21) sts.

Work even until piece measures same as back to shoulder shaping, ending with RS row.

Shape Shoulder

Next row (WS): BO 5 (5, 5, 7) sts at beg of row.

Work 1 row even.

BO 6 (7, 7, 7) sts at beg of next row.

Work 1 row even.

BO rem 6 (7, 7, 7) sts.

SLEEVES (make 2)

With smaller needles, CO 43 (43, 45, 45) sts.

Work in double moss st for 1½".

Change to larger needles and cont in double moss st. Work 4 rows.

Inc 1 st at each end of next and foll 4th rows 18 (18, 19, 19) times—81 (81, 85, 85) sts.

Work even until sleeve measures 18" (all sizes).

Shape Sleeve Cap

BO 4 sts at beg of next 2 rows.

BO 2 sts at beg of next 16 (16, 18, 18) rows.

BO rem 41 sts (all sizes).

FINISHING

Sew shoulder seams.

Set in sleeves.

Sew side and sleeve seams.

Neckband: With RS facing you and beg at right front neck shaping, PU 27 (27, 31, 31) sts up right front neck, 41 sts across back neck, and 27 (27, 31, 31) sts up left front neck—95 (95, 103, 103) sts. Knit 1 row. BO all sts knitwise.

Sew hook and eye to each side of neckband to close front neck edge.

Steam seams lightly if desired.

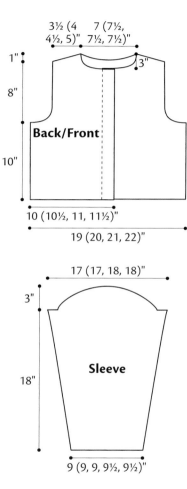

CHAPTER 4

Buttonholes

Nothing adds a professional touch to a finished garment like neat and tidy buttonholes. You can make different types of knitted buttonholes, depending on the size of your buttons and the gauge of your knitting.

YARN-OVER BUTTONHOLE

A yarn-over buttonhole is a small buttonhole that always looks neat.

1. Work to the point in your knitting where the buttonhole is to be.
2. (K2tog, YO), finish row; or (YO, K2tog), finish row (fig. 31).
3. On the next row, knit or purl into the YOs as required to maintain your pattern stitch (fig. 32). See figure 33 for finished buttonhole.

BIND-OFF BUTTONHOLE

A bind-off buttonhole creates a larger buttonhole than a simple yarn over.

1. Work to the point in your knitting where the buttonhole is to be.
2. Bind off the required number of stitches; finish row.
3. On next row, when you get to the "hole," cast on the same number of stitches that were bound off, using the backwards loop method (see page 18).

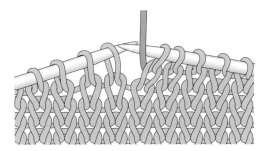

Yarn over needle on right side.
Fig. 31

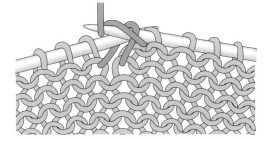

Purl yarn over on next row.
Fig. 32

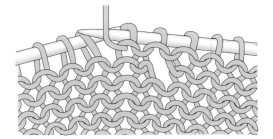

Finished buttonhole as seen from wrong side.
Fig. 33

Triangle Purse

This one-piece purse is a great way to practice your yarn overs. Make sure you do not knit into the back of the yarn overs as this will close up the hole. As a rule of thumb, if it is hard to knit the yarn overs, you are doing it wrong! For a correct yarn over, the yarn should come from the back of your work, between the needles, over the right needle, to the back of the work again.

Skill Level: Easy ◖■■☐▷

Finished Size: 8" wide x 9½" tall (excluding strap)

MATERIALS

MC: 1 hank of Recycled Silk from Himalaya Yarn (100% silk; 100 g, 80 yds), assorted colors (each hank is unique) (⑤)

CC: 1 hank of Glacé from Berroco (100% rayon; 1¾ oz, 50 g; 75 yds, 69 m) color 2571 Sprout (④)

Size 8 (5 mm) needles or size required to obtain gauge

2 size 6 (4 mm) double-pointed needles (dpn)

1 button, ¾"

Sewing needle and matching thread

GAUGE

14 sts and 20 rows = 4" in St st

I-CORD

Using dpn, CO 4 sts.

Row 1: Knit 1 row.

Row 2: Do not turn, slide sts to other end of needle, K4.

Rep row 2 until cord is desired length.

DIRECTIONS

With MC and size 8 needles, CO 4 sts.

Row 1 (RS): Knit.

Row 2: Purl.

Row 3: K2, YO, K2.

Row 4: Purl.

Row 5: K2, YO, knit to last 2 sts, YO, K2.

Row 6: Purl.

Rep rows 5 and 6 until you have about 3 yards of yarn left. (**Hint:** One yard is about an arm's length.)

BO all sts.

FINISHING

Thoroughly wet triangle and pin flat to dry.

Cut 4 strands of CC, each about 1 yard long.

Weave all 4 strands of contrast yarn through the holes made with YOs.

Weave in ends on inside of purse.

Fold bound-off edge in thirds (A to A and B to B as in diagram below) and sew together along the bottom edge.

Fold CO edge over and sew button to correspond to first YO, making sure to sew button through both layers of knitting.

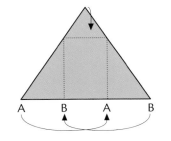

Using thread, tack down outside flap of purse.

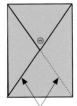

Tack here.

Handle

Using CC and dpn, knit I-cord for 36" or desired length.

BO all sts.

Sew strap to purse, using thread.

Woven contrasting yarn matches the purse handle.

Mock-Rib Cardigan

Since every other row is just knit, you can whip up this beauty in no time. This sweater is designed with three-quarter-length sleeves knit from the top down to the cuff. If you would like to lengthen the sleeves, when you have reached the pattern measurement, try the sweater on and continue knitting until you have reached the desired length. Find a great button from your grandmother's collection and you have a work of art.

Skill Level: Easy ◖■□□

Finished Bust: 40 (42, 44, 46, 48, 50)" when buttoned
Finished Length: 21 (21, 22, 22, 23, 23)"

MATERIALS

7 (7, 8, 8, 8, 8) balls of Suede from Berroco (100% nylon; 1¾ oz, 50 g; 120 yds, 111 m), color 3727 Dale Evans (cream) ❨4❩

9 (9, 10, 10, 11, 11) balls of Glacé from Berroco (100% rayon; 1¾ oz, 50 g; 75 yds, 69 m), color 2001 Vanilla ❨4❩

Size 13 (9 mm) needles or size required to obtain gauge

Size 11 (8 mm) needles

1 button, approx 1"

Sewing needle and matching thread

GAUGE

13 sts and 16 rows = 4" in mock rib using larger needles and 1 strand of A and 1 strand of B held tog

MOCK-RIB PATTERN

(worked over odd number of stitches)

Row 1 (RS): Knit.

Row 2: K1, *P1, K1*; rep from * to * to end of row.

Rep rows 1 and 2 for patt.

BACK

With smaller needles and double strand of A, CO 67 (69, 73, 75, 79, 81) sts.

Knit 4 rows.

Next row (RS): Change to larger needles. With 1 strand of A and 1 strand of B held tog, work row 1 in mock-rib patt.

Work even in mock-rib patt until piece measures 13", ending with WS row.

Shape Armhole

BO 6 sts at beg of next 2 rows—55 (57, 61, 63, 67, 69) sts.

Work even until armhole measures 8 (8, 9, 9, 10, 10)", ending with RS row. Piece should measure 21 (21, 22, 22, 23, 23)".

Shape Shoulders

BO 5 (6, 7, 7, 7, 8) sts at beg of next 2 rows.

BO 5 (6, 6, 6, 7, 8) sts at beg of next 2 rows.

BO 5 (5, 6, 6, 7, 7) sts at beg of next 2 rows.

BO rem 25 (23, 23, 25, 25, 23) sts.

LEFT FRONT

With smaller needles and double strand of A, CO 33 (35, 37, 37, 39, 41) sts.

Knit 4 rows.

Next row (RS): Change to larger needles. With 1 strand of A and 1 strand of B held tog, work row 1 of mock-rib patt.

Work even in mock-rib patt until piece measures 13", ending with WS row.

Shape Armhole

Next row (RS): BO 6 sts at beg of next row— 27 (29, 31, 31, 33, 35) sts.

Work 1 row even.

Shape V-neck

Row 1 (dec row, RS): Knit to last 4 sts, K2tog, K2.

Row 2: P1, *(P1, K1)*; rep from * to * to last st, P1.

Row 3 (dec row): Rep row 1.

Row 4: P2, *(P1, K1)*; rep from * to * to last st, P1.

Rep last 4 rows 5 more times—15 (17, 19, 19, 21, 23) sts.

Work even in mock rib until piece measures same as back to shoulder shaping, ending with WS row.

Shape Shoulder

Next row (RS): BO 5 (6, 7, 7, 7, 8) sts at beg of row.

Work 1 row even.

BO 5 (6, 6, 6, 7, 8) sts at beg of next row.

Work 1 row even.

BO rem 5 (5, 6, 6, 7, 7) sts.

RIGHT FRONT

With smaller needles and double strand of A, CO 33 (35, 37, 37, 39, 41) sts.

Knit 4 rows.

Next row (RS): Change to larger needles. With 1 strand of A and 1 strand of B held tog, work row 1 of mock-rib patt.

Work even until piece measures 13", ending with RS row.

Shape Armhole

Next row (WS): BO 6 sts at beg of row—27 (29, 31, 31, 33, 35) sts.

Shape V-neck

Row 1 (dec row, RS): K2, ssk, knit to end of row.

Row 2: *(P1, K1)*; rep from * to * to last 2 sts, P2.

Row 3 (dec row): Rep row 1.

Row 4: *(P1, K1)*; rep from * to * to last 3 sts, P3.

Rep last 4 rows 5 more times—15 (17, 19, 19, 21, 23) sts.

Work even in mock-rib patt until piece measures same as back to shoulder shaping, ending with RS row.

Shape Shoulder

Next row (WS): BO 5 (6, 7, 7, 7, 8) sts at beg of row.

Work 1 row even.

BO 5 (6, 6, 6, 7, 8) sts at beg of next row.

Work 1 row even.

BO rem 5 (5, 6, 6, 7, 7) sts.

Sew shoulder seams.

SLEEVES (make 2)

With larger needles and 1 strand of A and 1 strand of B held tog, PU 53 (53, 59, 59, 65, 65) sts between armhole bind offs.

Beg with row 2 of patt, work in mock rib for 3", ending with WS row.

Dec 1 st at each end of next and foll 4th rows 10 (10, 11, 11, 13, 13) times—31 (31, 35, 35, 37, 37) sts rem.

Work even until sleeve measures 16" or desired length, ending with RS row.

Change to smaller needles and double strand of A. Knit 4 rows.

BO all sts loosely.

FINISHING

Button band: With RS facing you, smaller needles, double strand of A, and beg at right front bottom edge, PU 72 (72, 76, 76, 80, 80) sts to right shoulder seam, then 25 (23, 23, 25, 25, 23) sts across back neck—97 (95, 99, 101, 105, 103) sts. Knit 2 rows. BO all sts loosely.

Buttonhole band: With RS facing you, smaller needles, double strand of A, and beg at left shoulder seam, PU 72 (72, 76, 76, 80, 80) sts to bottom left edge.

Next row (buttonhole): Knit 40, BO 2 sts, knit to end.

Knit next row, CO 2 sts over bound-off sts.

BO all sts loosely.

Sew top 2" of sleeve to bound-off edges at armhole. Sew sleeve to armhole.

Sew side and sleeve seams.

Sew on button to correspond with buttonhole.

Sew button band to buttonhole band at left shoulder.

Steam seams lightly if desired.

Work decreases in from edge to create smooth shaping.

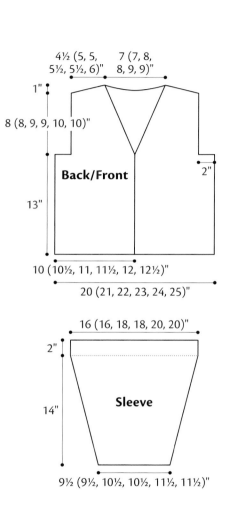

4½ (5, 5, 5½, 5½, 6)"   7 (7, 8, 8, 9, 9)"

1"

8 (8, 9, 9, 10, 10)"

Back/Front

2"

13"

10 (10½, 11, 11½, 12, 12½)"

20 (21, 22, 23, 24, 25)"

16 (16, 18, 18, 20, 20)"

2"

14"

Sleeve

9½ (9½, 10½, 10½, 11½, 11½)"

Color Knitting (Intarsia)

Working with more than one color of yarn can make an exciting project. You can do this by using a contrast color for edgings or trims, or by using more than one color in the knitting itself. One method of using multiple colors is called "intarsia," where the colors are connected by twisting yarns on the back of the work. Yarns are not carried or stranded across the back of the knitting as they are in Fair Isle knitting. In this book, we'll focus specifically on intarsia color work.

USING BOBBINS

Bobbins can be used to hold small quantities of each color, to help keep the yarns from tangling. You may use commercially available bobbins or make your own. To create your own bobbin:

1. Wrap yarn around your index finger.

2. Make figure eights around your thumb and little finger.

3. Cut the yarn and wrap it around the middle of the "eights" twice, then pull it through.

4. Knit with the yarn end that was wrapped around your index finger.

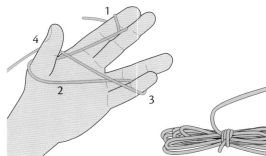

Wrap yarn around thumb and little finger.

Cut end and secure around yarn.

READING COLOR CHARTS

Color designs are usually worked according to a chart. Each square in the chart represents a stitch to be worked in the designated color. Some patterns will write out each row of the pattern and some patterns will use both a chart and written instructions.

Unless otherwise specified in the pattern, charts should be worked from right to left on RS rows and left to right on WS rows.

CASTING ON IN INTARSIA

When working in intarsia, you may need to cast on with several colors across the row.

1. Cast on the required number of stitches for first color using long-tail cast on.

2. Make a slipknot with second color and place on needle after first-color stitches. This counts as a stitch.

3. Twist yarns on the back of the work to prevent a hole.

4. Cast on the required number of stitches with second color using long-tail cast on.

Repeat this process with all of the colors used in the first row of knitting.

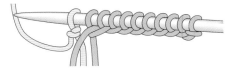

Put slipknot with new color on needle. Bring new color under old color.

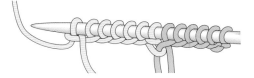

Cast on with new color.

KNITTING IN INTARSIA

Work colors according to chart or pattern.

To prevent holes in the knitting, make sure to twist yarns at the back of the work whenever you change colors by bringing the new yarn under the old yarn and into position for the next stitch.

Make sure yarns are on the wrong side of your work when twisting them.

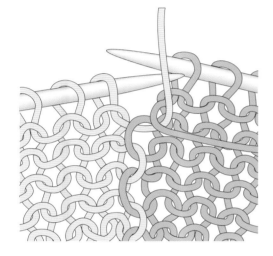

PURLING IN INTARSIA

When you purl in intarsia color work, the wrong side is facing you; therefore the yarns are in the front of the work when they are twisted.

ADDING A NEW COLOR

At certain points during your knitting, you will need to add a new color.

1. Work to the stitch that requires a new color.

2. Knit one stitch with the new color.

3. Bring the new color under the old color and work the next stitch.

WEAVING IN ENDS

When weaving in ends in color knitting, weave each end into its respective color patch.

BINDING OFF IN INTARSIA

Bind off as you normally would work a row of color knitting, twisting yarns to prevent gaps in the bound-off edge.

Intarsia Purse

A small project to propel you into the world of color work, this purse is perfect for everyday use. The front and back are knit in different color patterns to give you experience in diagonal and straight color changes. For a larger purse, substitute a bulkier yarn and bigger needles.

Skill Level: Intermediate ⬤■■☐

Finished Size: 1¾" deep x 9" wide x 6" tall (excluding strap)

MATERIALS

1 ball each in the following colors of All Seasons Cotton from Rowan (60% cotton, 40% acrylic; 50 g; 98 yds, 90 m): (**4**)

MC: color 213 Military Green

CC1: color 203 Giddy

CC2: color 182 Bleached

Size 7 (4.5 mm) needles or size required to obtain gauge

1 button, ¾"

Sewing needle and matching thread

NOTE: Pink lines on chart (page 55) indicate where a new ball of yarn will be added to the work. Since yarns are not carried across the back of the work, you may need multiple balls of the same color to complete a row of the chart. The yardages indicated are the approximate length of yarn required for the bobbin of that color.

GAUGE

20 sts and 28 rows = 4" in St st

SEED STITCH

(worked over odd number of sts)

All rows: *K1, P1*; rep from * to * to last st, K1.

DIRECTIONS

CO 56 sts with MC.

> **Row 1 (RS):** (K1, P1) 4 times, K40, (P1, K1) 4 times.
>
> **Row 2:** (K1, P1) 4 times, P40, (P1, K1) 4 times.

Rep rows 1 and 2 twice more.

Keeping first and last 8 sts in seed st as est and joining in and breaking off colors as indicated, follow chart on page 55 through row 42.

NOTE: The chart indicates the length of yarn required for each color patch. Wind off bobbins of yarn as indicated in chart. If the chart indicates "ball," it is not necessary to use a bobbin, just use the entire ball of yarn.

BO 8 sts at beg of next 2 rows—40 sts.

Cont in MC and seed st for 10 rows, inc 1 st at each end of last row—42 sts.

Cont chart through row 94. BO all stitches.

Back of Intarsia Purse

A seed-stitch border keeps the purse stable at its bottom edge.

FINISHING

Sew bound-off stitches to seed-st section.

Sew side seams.

Steam seams lightly if desired.

Using CC1, crochet 1 row of sl st (see page 27) all around top of purse, making button loop in middle of one side as follows:

At button placement, chain 10 and skip 1 st.

Handles

With MC, CO 7 sts, leaving a 12" tail for sewing.

Work in seed st for 4½".

Work in St st for 5".

Work in seed st for 4½".

BO all sts, leaving a 12" end for sewing.

Attach handles inside sl-st row.

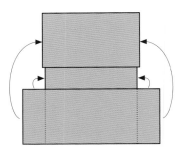

Bring ends together
and sew seams.

Pink lines indicate where to
start each new ball of yarn.

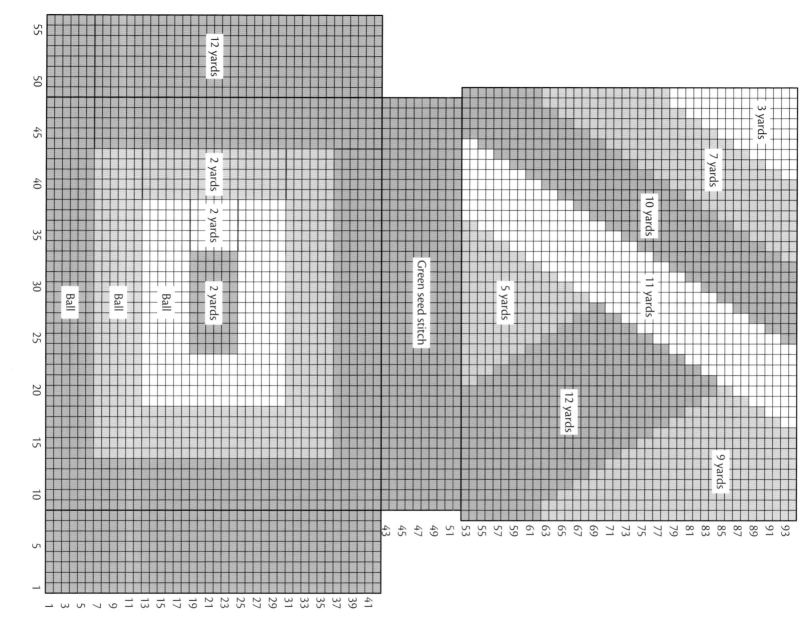

Asymmetric-Band Jacket

Knitting this jacket is a great way to determine if you like the intarsia method of color work. Simple color blocks on the cuffs and buttonhole band are an interesting introduction to this technique. If you have a button collection, find seven of your favorites and make this a one-of-a-kind garment. Included in this design are set-in sleeves and simple shaping at the waist to create flattering lines.

Skill Level: Intermediate ■■■□

Finished Bust: 38 (40, 42, 44)" when buttoned
Finished Length (all sizes): 23"

MATERIALS

MC: 13 (13, 14, 14) balls of Kashmir Aran from Louisa Harding (55% merino wool, 35% microfiber, 10% cashmere; 50 g; 83 yds, 75 m), color 12 (gray) ④

A: 1 ball of Kashmir Aran from Louisa Harding, color 7 (blue) ④

B: 1 ball of Impression from Louisa Harding (84% nylon, 16% mohair; 50 g; 154 yds, 140 m), color 7 (teals and blues) ④

C: 1 ball of Kimono Ribbon from Louisa Harding (100% nylon; 50 g; 102 yds, 92 m), color 3 (browns) ④

D: 1 ball of Impression, color 8 (tans) ④

E: 1 ball of Kimono Angora from Louisa Harding (70% angora, 25% wool, 5% nylon; 25 g; 124 yds, 112 m), color 3 (tans and browns) ④

F: 1 ball of Kimono Ribbon, color 10 (blues) ④

G: 1 ball of Kashmir Aran, color 5 (teal) (G) ④

Size 9 (5.5 mm) needles or size required to obtain gauge in St st with MC

Size 6 (4 mm) needles or size required to obtain gauge in seed st with A

Size 8 (5 mm) needles

7 buttons, ½" or ¾"

7 pairs of hooks and eyes

Sewing needle and matching thread

GAUGE

18 sts and 24 rows = 4" in St st using MC and largest needles

20 sts and 30 rows = 4" in seed st using A and smallest needles

SEED STITCH

(worked over odd number of sts)

All rows: *(K1, P1)*; rep from * to * to last st, K1.

BACK

With middle-sized needles and MC, CO 85 (91, 95, 99) sts.

Work in seed st for 4 rows.

Change to largest needles and St st. Beg with a knit row, work 10 rows.

Next row (dec row, RS): K3, K2tog, knit to last 5 sts, ssk, K3.

Work 7 rows even.

Rep last 8 rows twice more and then rep dec row once more—77 (83, 87, 91) sts.

Work even for 13 rows.

Next row (inc row, RS): K3, M1, knit to last 3 sts, M1, K3.

Work 7 rows even.

Rep last 8 rows 3 more times—85 (91, 95, 99) sts.

Work even until piece measures 14½ (14½, 14, 14)".

Shape Armhole

BO 3 sts at beg of next 2 rows.

Next row (RS): K3, K2tog, knit to last 5 sts, ssk, K3.

Next row (WS): Purl.

Rep last 2 rows 4 more times—69 (75, 79, 83) sts.

Work even until armhole measures 8½ (8½, 9, 9)".

Shape Shoulders

BO 8 sts at beg of next 4 rows.

BO 7 sts at beg of next 2 rows.

BO rem 23 (29, 33, 37) sts.

LEFT FRONT

With middle-sized needles and MC, CO 43 (45, 47, 49) sts.

Work in seed st for 4 rows.

Change to largest needles and St st. Beg with a knit row, work 10 rows.

Next row (dec row, RS): K3, K2tog, knit to end.

Work 7 rows even.

Rep last 8 rows twice more and then rep dec row once more—39 (41, 43, 45) sts.

Work even for 13 rows.

Next row (inc row, RS): K3, M1, knit to end.

Work 7 rows even.

Rep last 8 rows 3 more times—43 (45, 47, 49) sts.

Work even until piece measures 14½ (14½, 14, 14)", ending with WS row.

Shape Armhole

Next row (RS): BO 3 sts at beg of row—40 (42, 44, 46) sts rem.

Next row (WS): Purl.

Next row: K3, K2tog, knit to end.

Rep last 2 rows 4 more times—31 (33, 35, 37) sts rem.

Work even until piece measures 21", ending with RS row.

Shape Neck and Shoulder

Next row (WS): BO 4 (5, 6, 7) sts, purl to end—27 (28, 29, 30) sts rem.

Cont to BO at neck edge on alt rows as follows:

BO 3 sts once, then 2 sts 1 (2, 3, 4) times, then 1 st 3 (2, 1, 0) times—23 sts rem for all sizes. AT THE SAME TIME, when piece measures same as back to beg of shoulder shaping, shape shoulder as follows:

BO 8 sts at beg of next 2 RS rows.

BO rem 7 sts.

RIGHT FRONT

With middle-sized needles and MC, CO 43 (45, 47, 49) sts.

Work in seed st for 4 rows.

Change to largest needles and St st. Beg with a knit row, work 10 rows.

Next row (dec row, RS): Knit to last 5 sts, ssk, K3.

Work 7 rows even.

Rep last 8 rows twice more and then rep dec row once more—39 (41, 43, 45) sts.

Work even for 13 rows.

Next row (inc row, RS): Knit to last 3 sts, M1, K3.

Work 7 rows even.

Rep last 8 rows 3 more times—43 (45, 47, 49) sts.

Work even until piece measures 14½ (14½, 14, 14)", ending with RS row.

Shape Armhole

Next row (WS): BO 3 sts at beg of row.

Next row (RS): Knit to last 5 sts, ssk, K3.

Next row: Purl.

Rep last 2 rows 4 more times—35 (37, 39, 41) sts.

Work even until piece measures 21", ending with WS row.

Shape Neck and Shoulder

Next row (RS): BO 4 (5, 6, 7) sts, knit to end.

Cont to BO at neck edge on foll alt rows as follows:

BO 3 sts once, then 2 sts 1 (2, 3, 4) times, then 1 st 3 (2, 1, 0) times—23 sts rem for all sizes. AT THE SAME TIME, when piece measures same as back to beg of shoulder shaping, shape shoulder as follows:

BO 8 sts at beg of next 2 WS rows.

BO rem 7 sts.

LEFT SLEEVE

NOTE: See page 50 for instructions on how to cast on with more than one color.

With smallest needles and A, CO 8 sts; cont to CO 10 sts with B, C, and D; CO 8 sts with E—46 sts.

Five of the seven yarns are used for each cuff.

Working colors as est and making sure to twist yarns on WS when changing colors to prevent holes, cont in seed st as follows:

Row 1: (K1, P1) to last st.
Row 2: (P1, K1) to last st.
Rep last 2 rows twice more.

Maintaining st patt and colors as est, inc 1 st at each end of next and foll 4th rows 3 times—54 sts.

Cont without shaping until cuff measures 2½", ending with WS row.

Change to MC and knit 1 row.

Change to largest needles and purl 1 row, dec 11 sts evenly across row—43 sts.

Cont in St st, inc 1 st at each end of 7th and foll 6th rows 9 (9, 10, 10) times—63 (63, 65, 65) sts.

Work even until sleeve measures 17" or desired length to armhole, ending with WS row.

Shape Cap

BO 3 sts at beg of next 2 rows.

Next row (dec row, RS): K3, K2tog, knit to last 5 sts, ssk, K3.

Rep dec row every other row 4 more times and then every 4th row twice—43 (43, 45, 45) sts.

BO 4 sts at beg of next 6 (6, 8, 8) rows.

BO rem 19 (19, 13, 13) sts.

RIGHT SLEEVE

Complete as for left sleeve, but use C, D, E, F, and G for cuff.

BUTTONHOLE BAND
(same for all sizes)

NOTES: The buttonhole band is worked in one piece using the intarsia technique. Make sure to twist each new color around the previous color on WS to prevent holes. See the note on page 10 for instructions on how to cast on at the end of a row.

With A and smallest needles, CO 15 sts.

Work 4 rows in seed st. CO 15 sts with B at end of last row.

Row 5 (RS): Work 15 sts in seed st with B, then work 15 sts in seed st with A.

Row 6 (WS): Work 15 sts in seed st with A, then work 15 sts in seed st with B.

Seven different yarns create this unique buttonhole band.

Row 7 (buttonhole, RS): Work 15 sts in seed st with B, work 7 sts in seed st with A, YO, K2tog, work 6 sts in seed st with A.

Row 8 (WS): Work 15 sts in seed st with A, work 15 sts in seed st with B, CO 15 sts with C at end of last row.

Row 9: Work 15 sts in seed st with C, 15 sts in seed st with B, 15 sts in seed st with A.

Row 10: Work 15 sts in seed st with A, 15 sts in seed st with B, 15 sts in seed st with C.

Row 11 (buttonhole, RS): Work 15 sts in seed st with C, work 7sts in seed st with B, YO, K2tog, work 6 sts in seed st with B, work 15 sts in seed st with A.

Row 12: Work 15 sts in seed st with A, 15 sts in seed st with B, 15 sts in seed st with C, then CO 15 sts with D at end of row.

Cont in this manner, adding 15 sts of next color (working in alphabetical order) at end of 4th row of preceding color and making a buttonhole on 7th row of each new color.

After all colors have been added and last buttonhole is made in color G, work 4 rows even on 105 sts.

BO all sts in patt with appropriate color, leaving an 8" tail of each color for sewing.

FINISHING

Using smallest needles, MC, and beg at bottom edge of right front, PU 85 sts evenly to beg of neck shaping.

Knit 1 row.

BO all sts.

Sew shoulder seams.

Neckband: With RS facing you, smallest needles, and MC, PU 16 (16, 18, 20) sts up right front neck edge, 25 (29, 31, 33) sts across back neck, 16 (16, 18, 20) sts down left front neck edge—57 (61, 67, 73) sts. Knit 1 row. BO all sts.

Sew bound-off edge of buttonhole band to left front.

Using thread and sewing needle, sew buttons to right front to correspond with buttonholes.

Using thread and sewing needle, sew eyes to right front edge to correspond with vertical placement of buttons.

Sew hooks to left front edge, at seam of buttonhole band and left front edge, to correspond with eyes on right front edge.

Fold sleeves in half and sew into armhole, matching middle of cap to shoulder seam.

Sew sleeve and side seams.

Steam seams lightly if desired.

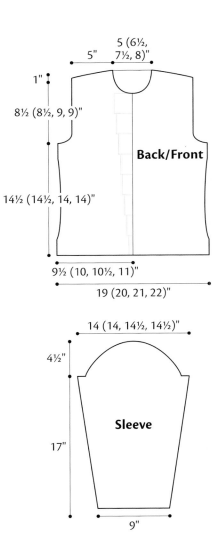

CHAPTER 6

New Stitches

There are only two stitches in knitting: the knit stitch and the purl stitch. But these can be combined in an infinite number of ways to create unique patterns. In this chapter, we will learn several different pattern stitches and discover how to use them in garments.

LINEN STITCH

Linen stitch requires a much larger needle size than called for on the yarn label. It has a compressed row gauge (about twice that of stockinette stitch) and a compressed stitch gauge (about the same as stockinette stitch using a smaller needle). Because of this, it can be used to make a very dense fabric. The stitch does not require you to use a selvage-stitch edge, because the pattern creates its own edge. This pattern is usually worked over an even number of stitches.

Basic Linen Stitch

(worked over even number of stitches)

Row 1 (RS): *Wyif, sl 1, K1*; rep from * to * to end of row.

Row 2 (WS): *Wyib, sl 1, P1*; rep from * to * to end of row.

Rep rows 1 and 2 for patt.

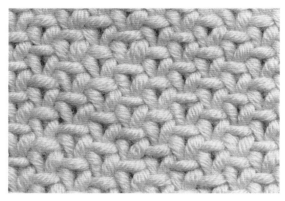

Basic linen stitch

Two-color linen stitch

Two-Color Linen Stitch

(worked over even number of stitches)

Row 1 (RS): With MC, *wyif, sl 1, K1*; rep from * to * to end of row.

Row 2: With MC, *wyib, sl 1, P1*; rep from * to * to end of row.

Row 3: With CC, *wyif, sl 1, K1*; rep from * to * to end of row.

Row 4: With CC, *wyib, sl 1, P1*; rep from * to * to end of row.

Rep rows 1–4 for patt.

Shaping in Linen Stitch

In linen stitch, increases and decreases are always worked in pairs to keep the pattern intact. Increases and decreases should always be done on row 1 of basic linen stitch, and they should always be worked over the top of a knit stitch, not a slipped stitch.

In addition to the decreases learned in chapter 2, the projects in this chapter use the following double increases and double decreases that add or remove two stitches at once.

Centered Double Decrease

With this decrease, the "middle" stitch will end up on top of the decrease.

ddec: Slip next 2 stitches as if to K2tog, knit next stitch, pass 2 slipped stitches over knit stitch.

Double Increase

This increase is similar to kfb (see page 17) with one more stitch added to it.

dinc: Knit into front, back, and front of next stitch.

Decrease Slanting to the Right

This decrease is similar to K2tog (see page 18) with one more stitch added to the decrease.

K3tog: Knit the next 3 stitches together.

Decrease Slanting to the Left

This decrease is similar to ssk (see page 18) with one more stitch added to the decrease.

sssk: Slip next 3 stitches as if to knit, one at a time, to right needle. Insert left needle in front of these stitches and knit them together.

Because sssk is sometimes difficult to knit in heavy yarn or if you knit tightly, the following is a nice alternative.

Sl 1, K2tog, psso: Slip next stitch as if to knit, knit two together (K2tog), pass slipped stitch over K2tog.

LOOP STITCH

The loop stitch makes a furry-looking fabric, with large loops of yarn sticking out from the surface of the knitting. It is usually worked on

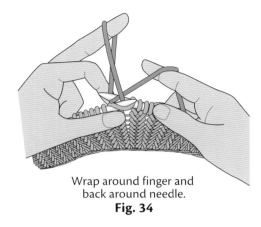

Wrap around finger and
back around needle.
Fig. 34

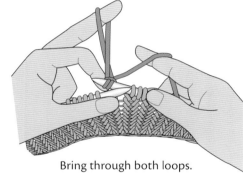

Bring through both loops.
Fig. 35

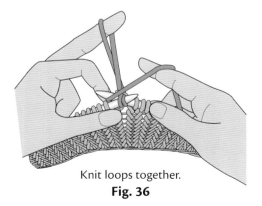

Knit loops together.
Fig. 36

wrong-side rows. Right-side rows are usually knitted plain.

Row 1 (WS): Knit 1, *insert needle into next stitch as if to knit, wrap yarn around needle, then clockwise around left middle finger, between finger and needle, around needle again (counter-clockwise; fig. 34), and pull through two loops (fig. 35). Insert left needle from left to right into these two stitches (in front of right needle), then knit two together (fig. 36)*; rep from * to * to last stitch, knit last stitch.

Row 2: Knit.

CABLES

Cables are a great way to add texture to any knitted garment. The actual process of knitting a cable is very simple. However, the more cables in a pattern, the more you need to be able to keep track of stitches and rows.

Cable Front

This cable will give the effect of stitches traveling over other stitches in a left-slanting direction.

1. Put stitches on a cable needle and hold to front of work.
2. Knit (or purl) the next stitches on the left needle.
3. Knit (or purl) the stitches on the cable needle.

This type of cable is usually abbreviated **CxxF**, where **xx** is the total number of stitches in the cable. You will only put some of these stitches on the cable needle.

EXAMPLE
Pattern reads C4F. Put 2 sts on cable needle and hold to front; K2, K2 from cable needle.

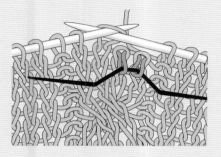

Bring sts on cable needle to front. Knit the next 2 sts.

Cable Back
This cable will give the effect of stitches traveling over other stitches in a right-slanting direction.

1. Put stitches on a cable needle and hold to back of work.
2. Knit (or purl) the next stitches on the left needle.
3. Knit (or purl) the stitches on the cable needle.

This type of cable is usually abbreviated **CxxB**, where **xx** is the total number of stitches in the cable. You will only put some of these stitches on the cable needle.

EXAMPLE
Pattern reads C4B. Put 2 sts on cable needle and hold to back; K2, K2 from cable needle.

Reading Cable Charts
Cables are usually worked according to a chart. Each square in the chart represents a stitch to be worked. Different symbols represent knits, purls, and cable twists. Some patterns will write out each row of the cable pattern and some patterns will use both a chart and written instructions.

Unless otherwise specified in the pattern, charts should be worked from right to left on right-side rows, left to right on wrong-side rows.

Translation of Chart
Row 1 (RS): K4, P1, K4, P1, K4, P1, K4, P1, K4, P1, K4.

Row 2: P4, K1, P4, K1, P4, K1, P4, K1, P4, K1, P4.

Row 3: K4, P1, C4B, P1, C4F, P1, C4B, P1, C4F, P1, K4.

Row 4: P4, K1, P4, K1, P4, K1, P4, K1, P4, K1, P4.

Rep rows 1–4 for cable pattern.

Notice that the cable row is only worked every fourth row; the rest of the time the cable stitches are worked in stockinette stitch.

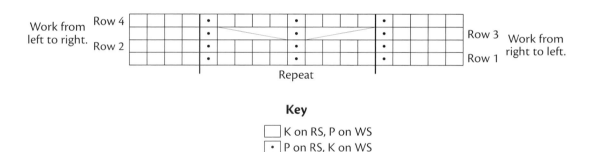

Work from left to right. Row 4 Row 2 Repeat Row 3 Row 1 Work from right to left.

Key

☐	K on RS, P on WS
⊡	P on RS, K on WS
⬲	C4B
⬳	C4F

No Horizontal Stripes for Me

Even being a "numbers" person, I thought this sweater was quite a challenge. When I was done and everything fit correctly, I told my husband it was a mathematical marvel. Unfortunately, all I got was a roll of his eyes! The Japanese yarn used to make this sweater creates the stripes on its own, which are vertical because the garment is worked from side to side rather than from bottom to top. This cardigan is also worked all in one piece, so the only sewing required is the side and underarm seams.

Skill Level: Experienced ◼◼◼▶

Finished Bust: 40 (44, 48, 52, 54, 58)" when buttoned
Finished Length: 25 (25, 26, 26, 27, 27)"

MATERIALS

5 (5, 6, 6, 7, 7) hanks of Silver Thaw from Noro (50% wool, 25% angora, 25% nylon; 100 g; 220 m) color 9 (multicolor) 🔅4🔅

Size 8 (5mm) circular needle (29" or longer) or size required to obtain gauge

2 spare needles or large stitch holders

2 stitch markers

Removable row markers or safety pins

5 large buttons, approx 1" or 1½"

Sewing needle and matching thread

GAUGE

17 sts and 26 rows = 4" in block patt

PATTERN STITCHES

Block Pattern

(multiple of 6 sts + 2)

Row 1 (RS): K2, *P4, K2*; rep from * to * to end of row.

Row 2 (WS): P2, *K4, P2*; rep from * to * to end of row.

Row 3: P2, *K4, P2*; rep from * to * to end of row.

Row 4: K2, *P4, K2*; rep from * to * to end of row.

Row 5: P2, *K4, P2*; rep from * to * to end of row.

Row 6: K2, *P4, K2*; rep from * to * to end of row.

Row 7: P2, *K4, P2*; rep from * to * to end of row.

Row 8: K2, *P4, K2*; rep from * to * to end of row.

Rep rows 1–8 for patt.

Linen Stitch

(multiple of 2 sts)

Row 1 (RS): *Wyif, sl 1, K1*; rep from * to * to end of row.

Row 2 (WS): *Wyib, sl 1, P1*; rep from * to * to end of row.

Rep rows 1 and 2 for patt.

LEFT SLEEVE

NOTE: This sweater is worked in one piece from left sleeve to right sleeve. Make sure you are very familiar with the block pattern as this sweater starts with a sleeve; you will be increasing in pattern almost immediately.

CO 44 (44, 50, 50, 56, 56) sts.

Work in linen stitch for 2", ending with WS row.

Next row (RS): Work row 1 of block patt.

Next row (WS): Work row 2 of block patt.

Cont working block pattern and AT THE SAME TIME inc 1 st at each end of next row, then inc 1 st at each end of every 6th row 15 (15, 16, 16, 17, 17) times—76 (76, 84, 84, 92, 92) sts.

Work even until sleeve measures 17 (18, 18, 18, 19, 19)", ending with WS row.

BODY

CO 70 sts (all sizes) at end of next 2 rows, working sleeve sts in est patt and new sts in St st—216 (216, 224, 224, 232, 232) sts.

Set up body patts as follows:

> **Rows 1, 5, and 7 (RS):** Work 10 sts in linen st, PM; beg with 3rd st of next row of block patt, work 196 (196, 204, 204, 212, 212) sts in block patt, PM, work 10 sts in linen st.

> **Rows 2, 4, 6, and 8(WS):** Work 10 sts in linen st, PM, work 196 (196, 204, 204, 212, 212) sts in block patt as est, PM, work 10 sts in linen st.

> **Row 3:** **Work 10 sts in linen st, turn**; rep from ** to ** once more, work 10 sts in linen st, work 196 (196, 204, 204, 212, 212) sts in block patt as est, work from ** to ** twice, work 10 sts in linen st.

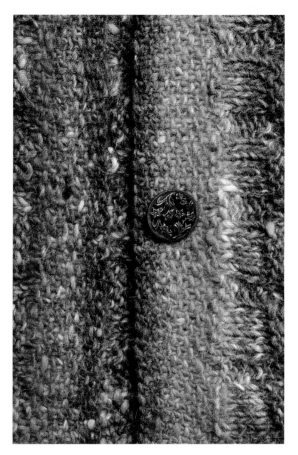

Linen stitch makes a very firm border for buttons.

NOTE: Row 3 of body pattern contains two extra short rows of the linen stitch to accommodate differences in gauge between the linen stitch and block pattern.

Cont in patts as est until body measures 6½ (7, 8, 9, 9½, 10½)", ending with WS row. PM on this row.

SEPARATE FOR NECK OPENING

Next row (RS): Cont in patts as est, work 108 (108, 112, 112, 116, 116) sts for back. Place rem sts on holder for front.

Cont on back sts only (making sure to work short rows on row 3 of patt at lower edge only), work even until back measures 6½ (7½, 7½, 7½, 8, 8)" from marker, ending with RS row.

Place back sts on holder.

LEFT FRONT

With RS facing, rejoin yarn to sts on holder.

Next row (RS): BO 4 sts at beg of row (neck edge). Cont in est block patt (making sure to work short rows on row 3 of patt at lower edge only).

Work 1 row even.

Next row: BO 3 sts at beg of row, work in patt to end.

Work 1 row even.

Next row: BO 2 sts at beg of row, work in patt to end.

Work 1 row even.

Next row: BO 1 st at beg of row, work in patt to end.

Work 3 rows even.

Rep last 4 rows once more.

Next row: BO 1 st at beg of row, work in patt to end—(96, 100, 100, 104, 104) sts.

Work 2 (4, 4, 4, 6, 6) rows even.

Next row (WS): Work 10 sts in linen st, remove marker, purl rem sts, inc 10 sts evenly spaced—

106 (106, 110, 110, 114, 114) sts.

Work 12 rows in linen st.

BO all sts in patt.

RIGHT FRONT

CO 106 (106, 110, 110, 114, 114) sts.

Work 6 rows of linen st over all sts.

Next row (buttonhole row): Work 3 sts in patt, **BO 3 sts, work until 21 (21, 22, 22, 23, 23) sts rem on needle**; rep from ** to ** 3 more times, BO 3 sts, work in patt to end.

Next row: Work in linen st, CO 3 sts over each buttonhole.

Cont in linen st for 5 more rows.

Next row (WS): Work first 10 sts in linen st, PM, purl across 96 (96, 100, 100, 104, 104) sts, dec 10 sts evenly spaced—96 (96, 110, 110, 104, 104) sts.

Next row (RS): Work in block patt to last 10 sts, work 10 sts in linen st.

Cont in patts as est (making sure to work short rows on row 3 of patt at lower edge only) for 1 (3, 3, 3, 5, 5) more rows.

CO 1 st at end of this row.

Work 4 rows even, CO 1 st at end of 4th row.

Rep last 4 rows twice more.

Work 2 rows even, CO 2 sts at end of 2nd row.

Work 2 rows even, CO 3 sts at end of 2nd row.

Work 2 rows even, CO 4 sts at end of 2nd row—108 (108, 112, 112, 116, 116) sts.

Work 1 row even; this is a RS row. PM on this row.

JOIN FRONTS TO BACK

Next row (WS): Cont in patts as est (making sure to work short rows on row 3 of patt on both edges), work across sts of right front and cont across all sts left on holder for back—216 (216, 224, 224, 232, 232) sts.

Cont on these 216 (216, 224, 224, 232, 232) sts in patts as est until piece measures 6½ (7, 8, 9, 9½, 10½)" from last marker.

BO 70 sts (all sizes) at beg of next 2 rows—76 (76, 84, 84, 92, 92) sts.

Sleeve cuffs are also done in linen stitch.

RIGHT SLEEVE

Cont in block patt over all sts, dec 1 st at each end of 5th row.

Dec 1 st at each end of every 6th row 15 (15, 16, 16, 17, 17) times—44 (44, 50, 50, 56, 56) sts.

Work even until sleeve measures 15 (16, 16, 16, 17, 17)".

Change to linen st and work even for 2".

BO all sts in patt.

FINISHING

Neckband: With RS facing and beg 1" from front opening edge, PU 30 (32, 32, 32, 34, 34) sts up left front neck shaping, 40 (42, 42, 42, 44, 44) sts across back neck, and 30 (32, 32, 32, 34, 34) sts down right front neck shaping, ending 1" from front edge—100 (106, 106, 106, 112, 112) sts. Work all sts in linen st for 1". BO all sts in patt.

Sew side and sleeve seams.

Sew on buttons to correspond with buttonholes.

Steam seams lightly if desired.

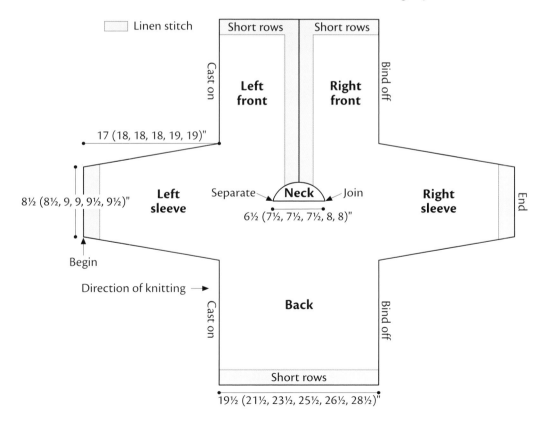

Linen stitch

Short rows | Short rows

Cast on

Left front | **Right front**

Bind off

17 (18, 18, 18, 19, 19)"

8½ (8½, 9, 9, 9½, 9½)"

Left sleeve

Separate — **Neck** — Join

6½ (7½, 7½, 7½, 8, 8)"

Right sleeve

End

Begin

Direction of knitting →

Cast on

Back

Bind off

Short rows

19½ (21½, 23½, 25½, 26½, 28½)"

Linen Stitch Shell

Silk and more silk are the keys to this amazing top. The style is perfect for anyone who does not have large shoulders. Its flattering shaping and cap sleeves make this shell wonderful under a jacket or all by itself. Linen stitch is a very slow stitch to knit. Take lots of breaks and persevere; it is worth every slipped stitch!

Skill Level: Experienced ◖■■■▶

Finished Bust: 36 (38, 40, 42, 44, 46)"
Finished Length: 22 (22, 23, 23, 24, 24)"

MATERIALS
MC: 3 (4, 4, 4, 5, 5) balls of Mulberry Silk from Laines Du Nord (100% silk; 1¾ oz, 50 g; 136 yds, 125 m) color 469 (taupe) (■3■)

CC: 2 hanks of Silk Delight from Great Adirondack (100% silk; 263 yds), color Rosewood (■3■)

Size 10 (6 mm) needles or size required to obtain gauge

Size 4 (3.5 mm) needles

Stitch holder or spare needle

GAUGE
24 sts and 36 rows = 4" in two-color linen st using larger needles

SHAPING TECHNIQUES
ddec (double decrease): Slip next 2 stitches as if to K2tog, knit next stitch, pass 2 slipped stitches over knit stitch (2 stitches decreased).

dinc (double increase): Knit into front, back, and front of next stitch (2 stitches increased).

TWO-COLOR LINEN STITCH

(worked over even number of sts)

Row 1 (RS): With MC, *wyif, sl 1, K1*; rep from * to * to end of row.

Row 2 (WS): With MC, *wyib, sl 1, P1*; rep from * to * to end of row.

Row 3: With CC, *wyif, sl 1, K1*; rep from * to * to end of row.

Row 4: With CC, *wyib, sl 1, P1*; rep from * to * to end of row.

Rep rows 1–4 for patt.

BACK AND FRONT (both alike)

NOTE: Do not cut yarn at end of row 2 or 4; carry yarn loosely up side of work. All ddecs and dincs should be worked on knit stitches, not slipped stitches (see page 62). BO sts in patt (see page 12).

Using MC and larger needles, CO 108 (114, 120, 126, 132, 138) sts.

Work in two-color linen st for 10 rows.

Next row (RS): Work 3 sts in patt, ddec, work in patt to last 5 sts, ddec, work 2 sts in patt.

Work 11 rows even (all sizes).

Rep last 12 rows twice more—96 (102, 108, 114, 120, 126) sts.

Work even until piece measures 8 (8, 9, 8½, 9, 9)", ending with row 2 or 4 of two-color linen st.

Next row (RS): Work 3 sts in patt, dinc, work in patt to last 3 sts, dinc, work 2 sts in patt.

Work 11 rows even.

The combination of solid and multicolored yarns are perfect in this stitch.

Rep last 12 rows twice more—108 (114, 120, 126, 132, 138) sts.

Work even until piece measures 14 (14, 15, 14½, 15½, 15½)", ending with row 2 or 4 of two-color linen st.

Shape Armhole

BO 5 sts at beg of next 2 rows.

NOTE: Rows will now start with a knit or purl stitch instead of a slipped stitch.

BO 2 sts at beg of next 12 rows—74 (80, 86, 92, 98, 104) sts.

Work even until armhole measures 2½" (all sizes), ending with row 2 or 4 of two-color linen st.

Shape Cap Sleeve

Next row (RS): Work 2 sts in patt, dinc in next st, work in patt to last 4 sts, dinc in next st, work 3 sts in patt.

Work 3 rows even.

Rep last 4 rows 7 more times—106 (112, 118, 124, 130, 136) sts.

Work even until armhole measures 6½ (6½, 6½, 7, 7, 7)", ending with row 2 or 4 of two-color linen st.

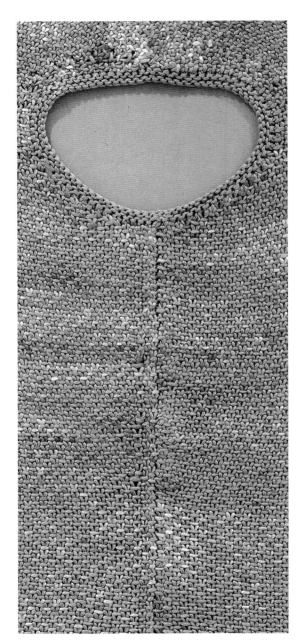

Increases and decreases are worked away from the seam to make a clean edge for sewing.

Shape Shoulders and Neck

Next row (RS): BO 2 sts at beg of row (shoulder edge), work 38 (42, 44, 47, 51, 53) sts in patt—39 (43, 45, 48, 52, 54) sts are on right needle.

Turn and place rem sts on holder or spare needle.

Left Shoulder

BO 3 sts at beg of next row (neck edge).

Cont in patt, BO 2 sts at shoulder edge 12 (8, 6, 6, 2, 0) more times.

BO 3 sts at shoulder edge 0 (4, 6, 6, 10, 12) times. AT THE SAME TIME, BO 3 sts at neck edge 4 (4, 4, 5, 5, 5) more times.

Fasten off last st.

Neck Center

With RS facing, place sts from holder onto working needle.

Reattach yarn and BO next 24 (22, 24, 24, 22, 24) sts, work in patt to end.

Right Shoulder

Next row (WS): BO 2 sts at beg of row (shoulder edge).

Next row (RS): BO 3 sts at beg of row (neck edge).

Cont in patt, BO 2 sts at shoulder edge 12 (8, 6, 6, 2, 0) more times.

BO 3 sts at shoulder edge 0 (4, 6, 6, 10, 12) times. AT THE SAME TIME, BO 3 sts at neck edge 4 (4, 4, 5, 5, 5) more times.

Fasten off last st.

FINISHING

Sew right shoulder seam.

Neckband: With RS facing you, smaller needle, and beg at left shoulder seam, PU 23 (23, 23, 26, 26, 26) sts down left front neck edge, 24 sts across front neck, 23 (23, 23, 26, 26, 26) sts up right front neck edge, 23 (23, 23, 26, 26, 26) sts down right back neck edge, 24 sts across back neck, 23 (23, 23, 26, 26, 26) sts up left back neck edge—140 (140, 140, 152, 152, 152) sts. Knit 2 rows. BO all sts knitwise.

Sew left shoulder seam, cont through neckband.

Armhole edges: With RS facing you and beg at armhole edge, PU 39 (39, 39, 42, 42, 42) sts up to shoulder seam and 39 (39, 39, 42, 42, 42) sts down to other armhole edge—78 (78, 78, 84, 84, 84) sts. Knit 2 rows. BO all sts knitwise.

Sew side seams and armhole bands.

Steam seams lightly, being careful not to stretch fabric.

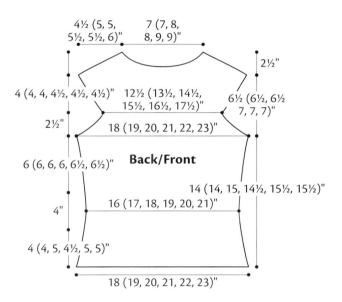

4½ (5, 5, 5½, 5½, 6)"   7 (7, 8, 8, 9, 9)"

2½"

4 (4, 4, 4½, 4½, 4½)"   12½ (13½, 14½, 15½, 16½, 17½)"   6½ (6½, 6½, 7, 7, 7)"

2½"   18 (19, 20, 21, 22, 23)"

6 (6, 6, 6, 6½, 6½)"   **Back/Front**

14 (14, 15, 14½, 15½, 15½)"

4"   16 (17, 18, 19, 20, 21)"

4 (4, 5, 4½, 5, 5)"

18 (19, 20, 21, 22, 23)"

Poodle Purse and Scarf

If your loops are not all the same size, don't worry; it adds to the design of the purse and scarf. The farther your finger is from the needle, the larger the loop will be. As with any ribbon, twisting is part of the game. If your yarn gets too twisted (starts to resemble thread), put a rubber band around the ball and hold your knitting in the air. The ball of yarn should untwist and become flat again. You may have to do this a few times in the course of knitting a ball of ribbon.

Skill Level: Intermediate ◀■■▶□

Purse Size: 8½" wide x 5½" tall (excluding strap)
Scarf Size: 99" long

MATERIALS
3 hanks of Segue from Trendsetter (100% polyamide; 3½ oz, 100 g; 120 yds, 110 m) color 603 Harvest (browns)* ⑤

*If you are making just the purse or scarf, you will need only 2 hanks of yarn.

Purse: Size 9 (5.5 mm) needles or size required to obtain gauge

Scarf: Size 13 (9 mm) circular needle at least 29" long

GAUGE
Purse: 12 sts and 20 rows = 4" in loop patt using smaller needles

Scarf: 10 sts = 4" in loop patt using larger needles

LOOP PATTERN

NOTE: See page 62 for instructions on making loops.

Row 1 (WS): K1, *loop 1*; rep from * to * to last st, K1.

Row 2 (RS): Knit.

Rep rows 1 and 2 for patt.

PURSE

With smaller needles, CO 51 sts.

Rep rows 1 and 2 of loop patt 6 times. Work row 1 once more.

Begin Shaping

Row 1 (dec row, RS): K2, K2tog, K18, K2tog, K3, K2tog, K18, K2tog, K2—47 sts.

Row 2 (and all WS rows through row 10): Work row 1 of loop patt.

Row 3: Knit.

Row 5 (dec row, RS): K2, K2tog, K16, K2tog, K3, K2tog, K16, K2tog, K2—43 sts.

Row 7 (RS): Knit.

Row 9 (dec row, RS): K2, K2tog, K14, K2tog, K3, K2tog, K14, K2tog, K2—39 sts.

Row 10: Work row 1 of loop patt.

BO all sts.

Fold purse in half and sew side and bottom seams.

Handle: CO 8 sts, work in St st for 10". BO all sts.

Sew handle onto purse.

Do not block because blocking will flatten the loop sts.

Loops are beautiful in a wide ribbon.

SCARF

NOTE: The scarf uses the loop stitch on both right-side and wrong-side rows. Work row 1 of loop pattern as instructed.

With larger needle, CO 200 sts.

Work row 1 of loop patt twice.

Work 1 more row of loop patt, binding off sts as row is worked.

Do not block because blocking will flatten the loop sts.

Diamonds and Cables

Simple rope cables and moss-stitch diamonds form a geometric design that is softened with an extraordinarily soft baby-alpaca yarn. Short garter-stitch borders make the most of the vertical lines created by the cables.

Skill Level: Intermediate ◼◼◼◻

Finished Bust: 38 (40, 42, 44, 48, 51)"
Finished Length: 23 (23, 23, 24, 24, 24)"

MATERIALS

9 (9, 10, 10, 11, 11) balls of Baby Alpaca Grande from Plymouth Yarn (100% baby alpaca; 100 g; 110 yds) color 3317 (green) ⑤

Size 10 (6 mm) needles or size required to obtain gauge

Size 9 (5.5 mm) needles

Size 9 (5.5 mm) circular needle, 16" long

Cable needle (cn)

GAUGE

14 sts and 22 rows = 4" in St st using larger needles

16 sts and 22 rows = 4" in chart patt using larger needles

CABLE STITCH

C4F: Slip 2 sts to cn, hold to front of work; K2, K2 from cn.

NOTE: On cable chart, odd rows are right-side rows and are read from right to left; even rows are wrong-side rows and are read from left to right. When increasing in a cable pattern, work the increased stitches in stockinette stitch until there are enough to work an entire cable plus one stitch to ensure that you are not working a cable at the very edge of your knitting.

BACK

With smaller needles, CO 76 (80, 84, 89, 96, 102) sts.

Knit 4 rows.

Change to larger needles and work from chart on page 78, beg and ending as indicated for your size.

Cont in patt as established until piece measures 15 (15, 14½, 15½, 15, 15)".

Shape Armhole

BO 8 sts at beg of next 2 rows—60 (64, 68, 73, 80, 86) sts.

Cont in chart patt as est, work until armhole measures 8, (8, 8½, 8½, 9, 9)".

Shape Back Neck and Shoulders

Next row (RS): BO 5 (5, 6, 6, 7, 8) sts at beg of row, work in patt until there are 14 (14, 14, 15, 16, 18) sts on right needle.

Diamonds are worked in knit-purl combinations.

Right Shoulder

Next row (WS): Turn work and BO 4 sts at beg of this row.

BO 5 (5, 5, 6, 6, 7) sts at beg of next row.

Work 1 row.

BO rem 5 (5, 5, 5, 6, 7) sts.

Neck Center

Next row (RS): With RS facing you, reattach yarn and BO center 22 (26, 28, 31, 34, 34) sts, work to end of row—19 (19, 20, 21, 23, 26) sts.

Left Shoulder

Next row (WS): BO 5 (5, 6, 6, 7, 8) sts at beg of row.

BO 4 sts at beg of next row.

BO 5 (5, 5, 6, 6, 7) sts at beg of next row.

Work 1 row.

BO rem 5 (5, 5, 5, 6, 7) sts.

FRONT

With smaller needles, CO 76 (80, 84, 89, 96, 102) sts.

Knit 4 rows.

Change to larger needles and work from chart on page 78, beg and ending as indicated for your size.

Cont in patt as est until piece measures 15 (15, 14½, 15½, 15, 15)".

Shape Armhole

BO 8 sts at beg of next 2 rows—60 (64, 68, 73, 80, 86) sts.

Cont in chart patt as est, work until armhole measures 6 (6, 6½, 6½, 7, 7)".

Shape Right Neck and Shoulder

Next row (RS): Work 22 (22, 23, 24, 26, 29) sts in patt, BO next 16 (20, 22, 25, 28, 28) sts, work to end of row.

Work 1 row even.

BO 3 sts at beg of next row.

Work 1 row even.

BO 2 sts at beg of next row.

Work 1 row even.

BO 1 st at beg of next row.

Work 1 row even.

Rep last 2 rows once more—15 (15, 16, 17, 19, 22) sts.

Work until piece measures same as back to shoulder shaping, ending with RS row.

Next row (WS): BO 5 (5, 6, 6, 7, 8) sts at beg of row.

Work 1 row.

BO 5 (5, 5, 6, 6, 7) sts at beg of next row.

Work 1 row.

BO rem 5 (5, 5, 5, 6, 7) sts.

Shape Left Neck and Shoulder

With RS facing you, reattach yarn to armhole edge and work to end of row.

Next row (WS): BO 3 sts at beg of row.

Work 1 row even.

BO 2 sts at beg of next row.

Work 1 row even.

Cables are the simple rope variety.

BO 1 st at beg of next row.

Work 1 row even.

Rep last 2 rows once more—15 (15, 16, 17, 19, 22) sts.

Work even until piece measures same as back to shoulder shaping, ending with WS row.

Next row (RS): BO 5 (5, 6, 6, 7, 8) sts at beg of row.

Work 1 row.

BO 5 (5, 5, 6, 6, 7) sts at beg of next row.

Work 1 row.

BO rem 5 (5, 5, 5, 6, 7) sts.

SLEEVES (make 2)

With smaller needles, CO 36 (36, 38, 38, 40, 40) sts.

Knit 4 rows.

Change to larger needles and work from chart on page 78, beg and ending as indicated for your size.

Keeping patt correct, inc 1 st at each end of next and every foll 6th row 4 times—46 (46, 48, 48, 50, 50) sts.

Work 5 rows even.

Inc 1 st at each end of next and every foll 4th row 9 (9, 10, 10, 11, 11) times—66 (66, 70, 70, 74, 74) sts.

Work even until sleeve measures 20".

Shape Sleeve Cap

BO 6 sts at beg of next 8 rows (all sizes).

BO rem 18 (18, 22, 22, 26, 26) sts.

FINISHING

Sew shoulder seams.

Neckband: With RS facing, circular needle, and beg at right shoulder seam, PU 30 (34, 36, 39, 42, 42) sts from back neck, 12 sts down left front neck shaping, 16 (20, 22, 25, 28, 28) sts from front neck, and 12 sts up right front neck shaping—70 (78, 82, 88, 94, 94) sts. Join in a round.

Purl 1 rnd. Knit 1 rnd. BO all sts purlwise.

Set in sleeves, sewing top 2" of sleeve into bound-off edge of armhole shaping.

Sew side and sleeve seams.

Steam seams lightly if desired.

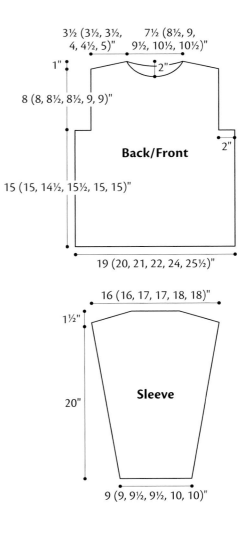

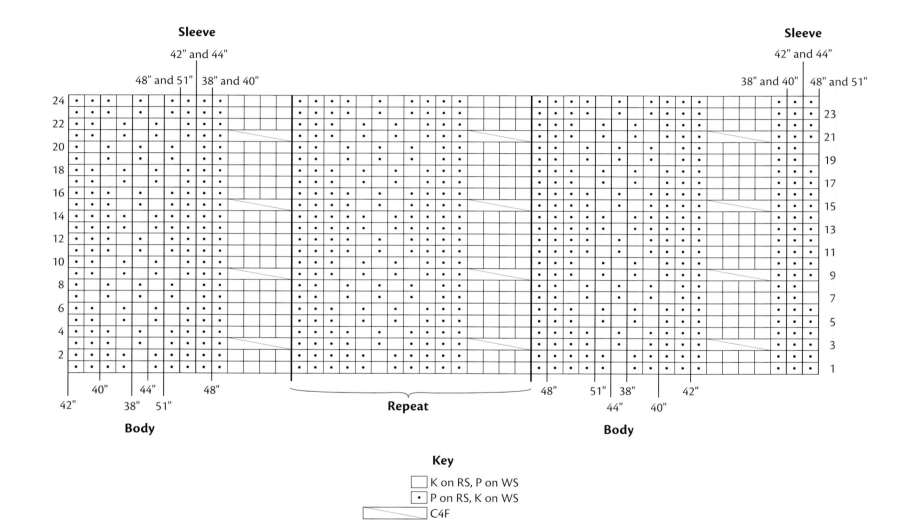

Key

	K on RS, P on WS
•	P on RS, K on WS
╱	C4F

Beads in Knitting

Beads add sparkle and shimmer to your knitting. They are easy to add to any knitted piece.

THREADING BEADS ONTO YARN

String beads onto your working yarn before you begin to knit. Thread about 20 grams of beads (1 tube) at a time unless pattern states otherwise. If you string too many beads at once, you will spend too much time sliding beads and not enough time knitting.

1. Thread a beading needle or a small sewing needle (must fit through bead) with about 4" of sewing thread.

2. Knot ends of the thread together.

3. Put yarn through this thread loop so that the end is doubled.

4. Slide beads onto the needle, then onto thread, and then onto yarn.

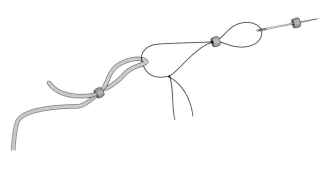

KNITTING WITH BEADS

Beads are slid down the working yarn toward the ball until they are ready to be knit. When a bead is to be knit into the row, slide it up close to the knitting. Project directions will indicate when to add a bead: Pb (place bead).

Pb as follows:

1. Bring yarn to front of work.

2. Slide bead close to right needle.

3. Slip next stitch purlwise.

4. Bring yarn to back of work.

5. Each bead should be "sitting" on top of the slipped stitch.

NOTES: Beads must be at least one stitch apart; you do not want to slip two stitches next to each other. Also, if you have heavily beaded knitting, be careful of your gauge; slipped stitches will make your knitting a little tighter.

FIXING MISTAKES IN BEADED KNITTING

If you are working a beaded pattern and find that you have added a bead where it shouldn't be, don't panic. Using a small set of pliers or tweezers, gently pull the bead away from your knitting. Using a small hammer, crack the bead and pull off the pieces. Be careful not to hit the bead too hard; you may not be able to find all of the pieces.

You also may find you have omitted a bead in the pattern. Simply take a needle and thread and sew the bead to your knitting in the correct place. The errant bead will be noticeable when you are sewing it, but when your project is finished, it will be hard to find.

Looped Beaded Purse

This purse combines loop stitch and beads. The design is fun to work and allows you to combine two unusual techniques to create one fantastic project.

Skill Level: Intermediate ■■■□

Finished Size: 6½" wide x 6¾" tall (excluding straps)

MATERIALS
MC: 1 hank of Clip from On Line (100% cotton; 100 g; 166 m), color 180 (teal green) ❹

CC: 1 Ball of Chinchilla Bulky from Berroco (100% rayon; 50 g; 41 yds), color 7505 Cumulus ❺

Approx 300 size 4 coordinating seed beads

Size 7 (4.5 mm) needles or size required to obtain gauge

2 size 7 (4.5 mm) double-pointed needles (dpn)

1 large snap or magnetic closure

GAUGE
21 sts and 26 rows = 4" in bead patt

PATTERN STITCHES
To place bead (Pb), see "Knitting with Beads" on page 79.

Loop Stitch
NOTE: See page 62 for instructions on making loops.

Row 1 (WS): K1, *loop 1*; rep from * to * to last st, K1.

Row 2 (RS): Knit.

Rep rows 1 and 2 for patt.

I-Cord

With dpn, CO 4 sts.

Knit 1 row.

Slide sts to other end of needle, K4; rep from * to * until desired length.

DIRECTIONS

Before beginning to knit, thread all beads onto MC (see page 79 for instructions).

Work Bottom Edging

Using MC, CO 72 sts. (CO edge is bottom edge of purse.)

Setup: Knit 1 row. Purl 1 row.

Row 1 (RS): K2, *Pb, K1*; rep from * to * to end of row.

Row 2: Purl.

Row 3: K1, *Pb, K1*; rep from * to * to last st, K1.

Row 4: Purl.

Rep these 4 rows twice more (end with a WS row).

Work Bag Sides

Rows 1 and 5 (RS): Knit.

Rows 2, 4, 6, and 8: Purl.

Row 3: K2, *Pb, K5*; rep from * to * to last 4 sts, Pb, K3.

Row 7: *K5, Pb*; rep from * to * to last 6 sts, K6.

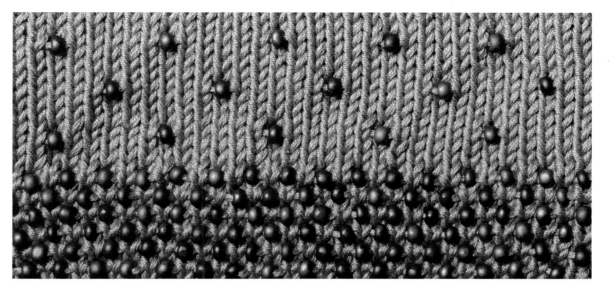

Beads are placed during the knitting.

Rep rows 1–8 three more times and then work rows 1–6 once.

Knit 1 row, dec 8 sts evenly spaced across row—64 sts.

Work 1½" in garter st, ending with RS row.

Next row (WS): Knit 1 row, dec 13 sts evenly spaced across row—51 sts.

Work Loop Trim

Change to CC.

Row 1 (RS): K1, *loop 1*; rep from * to * to last st, K1.

Row 2 (WS): Knit.

Rep rows 1 and 2 once more and then rep first row again.

BO all sts knitwise.

FINISHING

Using MC, make two I-cord handles, each approx 8" long.

Fold purse in half and sew side seam and bottom seam (CO edge).

Fold looped top over purse so loops are on outside of purse.

Sew handles to each side of purse, to last row of MC, about 2" from side seam.

Attach snap to inside edges of front and back of purse, between handles, and under loop border.

No blocking is necessary.

CHAPTER 8

Lace Basics

Many knitters are afraid of lace, thinking that it is difficult to knit. In reality, it is easier than some of the techniques you have already learned in this book. The following instructions will give you the confidence you need to try the two lace projects at the end of the chapter.

BASIC LACE STITCHES

The basic stitches in lace are the yarn over (an increase) and decreases. The yarn over is what makes the holes in lace knitting, while the decreases keep your stitch count correct and draw lines that accentuate the lace pattern in your knitting. When working into the yarn over on the following row, be sure not to twist the yarn, as this will close up the hole.

Yarn Over (YO)

Each time you create a yarn over by wrapping the yarn over the needle you will add one stitch to your total stitch count. It can be worked in four different ways, depending on the type of stitch before and after the yarn over.

1. *Stitch before is knit; stitch after is knit.* Bring yarn from back of knitting to front between needles and over the top of the right needle to the back again.
2. *Stitch before is knit; stitch after is purl.* Bring yarn to front of work between needles and completely around right needle to front of work.
3. *Stitch before is purl; stitch after is knit.* Bring yarn from front to back over right needle.
4. *Stitch before is purl; stitch after is purl.* Bring yarn completely around right needle to front again.

Decreases

To keep your stitch count correct, you will need to pair each yarn over with a decrease. Decreases can slant to the right or left, or they can be centered. Note that decreases do not necessarily have to be immediately next to the yarn overs; they can be spaced away from the yarn over, before or after it.

Right-slanting decreases include K2tog (see page 18) and K3tog (see page 62). Left-slanting decreases include ssk (see page 18); sssk; and sl 1, k2tog, psso (see page 62). A centered decrease is S2KP (see page 84). There are also other more esoteric decreases used in advanced lace-knitting patterns that are beyond the scope of this book.

Small flowers are a great first lace project (see Lace Scarf on page 84).

READING LACE CHARTS

Many lace patterns will have a chart to work from, and the chart will have a key for the symbols used. Each square in the chart represents one stitch in your knitting. The decrease symbols are generally over just one stitch, even though two stitches are used; the yarn over makes up for the other stitch.

Charts should be worked from right to left on right-side rows, left to right on wrong-side rows.

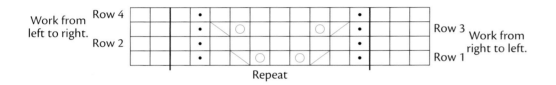

Work from left to right. — Row 4, Row 2

Row 3, Row 1 — Work from right to left.

Repeat

Key

☐	K on RS, P on WS
☐•	P on RS, K on WS
☐○	YO
☐╱	K2tog
☐╲	SSK

Translation of Chart

Row 1: K3, *P1, K1, K2tog, TO, K1, YO, ssk, K1, P1, K1*, **P1, K1, K2tog, TO, K1, YO, ssk, K1, P1, K1**, K2.

Row 2: Purl.

Row 3: K3, *P1, K2tog, YO, K3, YO, ssk, P1, K1*, **P1, K2tog, YO, K3, YO, ssk, P1, K1**, K2.

Row 4: Purl.

Rep rows 1–4 for lace pattern.

NOTE: The * to * and ** to ** are the repeats from the chart.

FIXING MISTAKES IN LACE KNITTING

If you discover that your stitch count is off or you have made a mistake in the pattern, you may have to rip some of your knitting. If the mistake is on the current row, take back the knitting one stitch at a time, being very careful to pick up any yarn overs from that row. If the mistake is farther down the knitting, it is still advisable to unknit only one stitch at a time until you are very comfortable with lace ripping.

In this book, each lace pattern consists of a lace row (RS) and a "rest" row (WS). The rest rows have no yarn overs and are mostly purled. For this reason, the easiest place to stop ripping and resume knitting is after a WS row.

SHAPING IN LACE KNITTING

When shaping in lace knitting, you must be very careful to keep the lace pattern continuous. If there are decreases or bind offs at the beginning or end of rows, make sure that all of your yarn overs and decreases are paired. If there are not enough stitches to complete a lace pattern repeat, work the extra stitches in stockinette stitch.

Lace Scarf

This scarf is a basic introduction to lacework. Each wrong-side row is a "resting" row; the entire row is purled. The lace pattern is worked according to the chart on the right-side rows. While you are knitting this scarf, it will curl at the edges. When you are finished, wet the scarf and lay it flat to dry, shaping gently with your fingers. If desired, you may use pins to obtain the correct shape. The scarf is worked in two pieces so that the flowers face the same way on both sides of your neck.

Skill Level: Intermediate ◼◼◼◻

Finished Size: 6½" wide x 50¾" long

MATERIALS
2 balls of Baby Alpaca D.K. from Plymouth Yarn (100% baby alpaca; 50 g; 125 yds) color 1837 (pink) 🧶**4**

Size 7 (4.5 mm) needles or size required to obtain gauge

3 removable markers or safety pins

Rustproof pins for blocking (optional)

GAUGE
20 sts and 28 rows = 4" in lace patt

DOUBLE DECREASE
S2KP: Slip next 2 sts as if to K2tog, K1, pass 2 slipped sts over.

HALF SCARF (make 2)
CO 33 sts.

Beg with a RS row, read chart row 1 from right to left.

Cont chart, noting that odd-numbered rows are RS rows and even-numbered rows are WS rows.

Work chart from rows 1–52.

Rep chart rows 29–52 four more times.

Work chart rows 53–76.

BO all sts.

FINISHING

Using row-to-row seaming (see page 20), sew halves of scarf together at bound-off edges. Thoroughly wet scarf.

Lay flat to dry, pinning if needed to obtain desired measurements.

Key

☐	K on RS, P on WS
•	P on RS, K on WS
○	YO
╲	K2tog
╱	SSK
⟨	S2KP

Chart columns (right to left, odd top): 75, 73, 71, 69, 67, 65, 63, 61, 59, 57, 55, 53, 51, 49, 47, 45, 43, 41, 39, 37, 35, 33, 31, 29, 27, 25, 23, 21, 19, 17, 15, 13, 11, 9, 7, 5, 3, 1

Chart columns (bottom, even): 76, 74, 72, 70, 68, 66, 64, 62, 60, 58, 56, 54, 52, 50, 48, 46, 44, 42, 40, 38, 36, 34, 32, 30, 28, 26, 24, 22, 20, 18, 16, 14, 12, 10, 8, 6, 4, 2

Beaded Lace Shell

This shell combines lace knitting with the bead knitting techniques from the previous chapter. The subtle interaction of lace and beads creates a design that is both elegant and delicate.

Skill Level: Experienced ■■■■◼

Finished Bust: 32 (35, 37, 40, 42, 46)"
Finished Length: 21 (21, 21½, 21½, 22, 22)"

MATERIALS

6 (6, 7, 7, 8, 8) hanks of Alpaca & Silk from Blue Sky Alpacas (50% alpaca, 50% silk; 50 g, 146 yds), color 10 Ecru 【2】

7 (7, 8, 8, 9, 9) tubes (each 20 g) of size 6 clear seed beads

Size 3 to 5 (3 mm to 3.75 mm) needles or size required to obtain gauge for size chosen (see below)

Stitch holders

GAUGE

28 sts and 40 rows = 4" in bead and lace patt for sizes 32 (37, 42)", using size 3 needles

26 sts and 36 rows = 4" in bead and lace patt for sizes 35 (40, 46)", using size 5 needles

NOTE: Due to the large number of stitches in one pattern repeat, some sizes are obtained by changing the gauge instead of the number of stitches. This garment is slightly fitted. Due to the nature of the knitting, there is some give in the fabric. When choosing your size, choose the size that is closest to your exact measurement.

BEAD AND LACE PATTERN

(multiple of 18 sts + 5)

To place beads (Pb), see page 79 for instructions. Before beginning to knit, thread 1 tube (approx 20 g) of beads onto yarn. When beads run out, break yarn and thread another tube of beads onto yarn.

NOTE: I have included the chart for this pattern on page 89 for those who prefer not to work from line-by-line instructions.

Row 1 (RS): K6, (Pb, K2tog, K2, YO, K1, YO, K2, ssk, Pb, K7) 5 (5, 6, 6, 7, 7) times, Pb, K2tog, K2, YO, K1, YO, K2, ssk, Pb, K6.

Rows 2, 4, and 6: Purl.

Row 3: K5, (Pb, K2tog, K2, YO, K3, YO, K2, ssk, Pb, K5) 5 (5, 6, 6, 7, 7) times, Pb, K2tog, K2, YO, K3, YO, K2, ssk, Pb, K5.

Row 5: K4, (Pb, K2tog, K2, YO, K5, YO, K2, ssk, Pb, K3) 5 (5, 6, 6, 7, 7) times, Pb, K2tog, K2, YO, K5, YO, K2, ssk, Pb, K4.

Row 7: K3, (Pb, K2tog, K2, YO, K2, P3, K2, YO, K2, ssk, Pb, K1) 5 (5, 6, 6, 7, 7) times, Pb, K2tog, K2, YO, K2, P3, K2, YO, K2, ssk, Pb, K3.

Row 8: P3, (P7, K3, P8) 5 (5, 6, 6, 7, 7) times, P7, K3, P10.

Row 9: K2, (Pb, K2tog, K2, YO, K3, P3, K3, YO, K2, ssk) 5 (5, 6, 6, 7, 7) times, Pb, K2tog, K2, YO, K3, P3, K3, YO, K2, ssk, Pb, K2.

Row 10: Purl.

BACK AND FRONT (both alike)

CO 113 (113, 131, 131, 149, 149) sts.

Work in bead and lace patt until piece measures 14" or desired length to underarm, ending with WS row.

Shape Armhole

BO 5 sts at beg of next 2 rows.

BO 2 sts at beg of next 2 (2, 4, 4, 8, 8) rows.

Dec 1 st at each end of every other row 4 (4, 6, 6, 6, 6) times.

Dec 1 st at each end of every 4th row twice—87 (87, 97, 97, 107, 107) sts rem.

Work even until armhole measures 6 (6, 6½, 6½, 7, 7)", ending with WS row.

Shape Neck and Shoulders

Next row (RS): Work 29 (29, 32, 32, 35, 35) sts in patt and place these sts on a holder. BO 29 (29, 33, 33, 37, 37) sts, work in patt to end.

First Side of Neck and Shoulder

Next row (WS): Work 1 row, ending at neck edge.

BO 4 sts at beg of next row.

Work 1 row even.

BO 3 sts at beg of next row.

Work 1 row even.

BO 2 sts at beg of next row.

Work 1 row even.

BO 1 st at beg of next row.

Work 1 row even.

Rep last 2 rows once more—18 (18, 21, 21, 24, 24) sts.

Work even until piece measures 21 (21, 21½, 21½, 22, 22)", ending with RS row.

Next row (WS): BO 6 (6, 7, 7, 8, 8) sts at beg of row.

Beads and lace combine in this elegant shell.

Work 1 row even.

Rep last 2 rows twice more. Fasten off last st.

Second Side of Neck and Shoulder

Place sts from holder on needle and complete second half of neck and shoulder as follows:

Next row (RS): Work 1 row, ending at neck edge.

BO 4 sts at beg of next row.

Work 1 row even.

BO 3 sts at beg of next row.

Work 1 row even.

BO 2 sts at beg of next row.

Work 1 row even.

BO 1 st at beg of next row.

Work 1 row even.

Rep last 2 rows once more—18 (18, 21, 21, 24, 24) sts.

Work even until piece measures 21 (21, 21½, 21½, 22, 22)", ending with WS row.

Next row (RS): BO 6 (6, 7, 7, 8, 8) sts at beg of row.

Work 1 row even.

Rep last 2 rows twice more. Fasten off last st.

FINISHING

Sew one shoulder seam (since the front and the back are alike, it does not matter which shoulder seam you sew).

Neck border: With RS facing you and beg at open shoulder edge, PU 22 sts down neck shaping, 29 (29, 32, 32, 35, 35) sts from bound-off neck edge, 22 sts up neck shaping, 22 sts down neck shaping, 29 (29, 32, 32, 35, 35) sts from bound-off neck edge, 22 sts up neck shaping—146 (146, 152, 152, 158, 158) sts. Knit 2 rows.

BO all sts knitwise. Sew second shoulder seam and neck border.

Armhole edges: With RS facing you and beg at armhole edge, PU 58 (58, 64, 64, 70, 70) sts to shoulder seam and 58 (58, 64, 64, 70, 70) sts to opposite armhole—116 (116, 128, 128, 140, 140) sts. Knit 2 rows. BO all sts knitwise.

Sew side seams.

Steam seams lightly if desired.

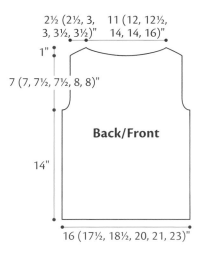

2½ (2½, 3, 3, 3½, 3½)"   11 (12, 12½, 14, 14, 16)"

1"

7 (7, 7½, 7½, 8, 8)"

Back/Front

14"

16 (17½, 18½, 20, 21, 23)"

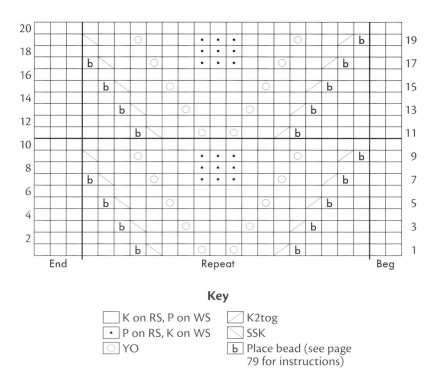

Key

☐ K on RS, P on WS	◨ K2tog
• P on RS, K on WS	◨ SSK
○ YO	b Place bead (see page 79 for instructions)

Mathematics

Don't be afraid of "knitter's math." You only need to know some basic arithmetic to get along with your knitting, and keeping a calculator handy will save you from working any calculations in your head or with a pencil and paper.

METRIC/ENGLISH CONVERSIONS

Meters (m) to yards (yds): Multiply by 1.0936 (you can use 1.1 for a quick approximation).

Yards (yds) to meters (m): Multiply by 0.9144 (you can use 0.9 for a quick approximation).

EXAMPLE

A ball of yarn is 100 meters and you need the measurement in yards. Multiply 100 by 1.0936 to get 109.36 yards in the ball.

A ball of yarn is 137 yards and you need the measurement in meters. Multiply 137 by 0.9144 to get 125.27 meters in the ball.

Centimeters (cm) to inches ("): Multiply by 0.3937 (you can use 0.4 for a quick approximation).

Inches (") to centimeters (cm): Multiply by 2.54 (you can use 2.5 for a quick approximation).

EXAMPLE

Your pattern says to work until piece measures 34 centimeters and you want inches.

Multiply 34 by 0.3937 to get 13.38 inches.

If you have a tape measure that has inches on one side and centimeters on the other side, you can use this to convert from imperial to metric measurements.

+ Measure on the side you are comfortable with.

+ Place a pin or your fingernail on the measurement.

+ Turn the tape measure to the other side and read the converted measurement.

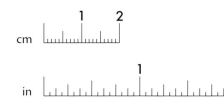

OTHER USEFUL CONVERSIONS

100 centimeters (cm) = 1 meter (m)

36 inches (") = 1 yard (yd)

1 ounce (oz) = 28.35 grams (g)

1 gram (g) = 0.0353 ounces (oz)

COMMON SIZES OF YARN BALLS

50 grams (g) = 1¾ ounces (oz)

100 grams (g) = 3½ ounces (oz)

4 ounces (oz) = 114 grams (g)

BUYING ENOUGH YARN

Always buy yarn by yardage unless you are using the exact yarn the pattern calls for. Never buy yarn by weight unless you are using the exact yarn the pattern calls for.

YARN USAGE

To calculate how much yarn is required for a project:

1. Multiply the number of yards in one ball of the yarn called for in your pattern by the number of balls called for in your pattern; this is the total yardage required for your project.

2. Divide this number by the number of yards in each ball of the yarn you will be using. This is the number of balls required to make the project. *Always* round up for the number of balls required.

EXAMPLE

Pattern calls for 17 balls of yarn, each 69 yards.

Total yardage required is 17 x 69 = 1173 yards.

Yarn you have chosen has 82 yards in each ball.

Number of balls of your yarn is 1173 ÷ 82 = 14.3.

You should buy 15 balls of yarn.

YARN WEIGHTS

Yarn-Weight Symbol and Category Names	1 Super fine	2 Fine	3 Light	4 Medium	5 Bulky	6 Super bulky
Types of Yarns in Category	Sock, Fingering, Baby	Sport, Baby	DK, Light Worsted	Worsted, Afghan, Aran	Chunky, Craft, Rug	Bulky, Roving
Knit Gauge Ranges in Stockinette Stitch to 4"	27 to 32 sts	23 to 26 sts	21 to 24 sts	16 to 20 sts	12 to 15 sts	6 to 11 sts
Recommended Needle in Metric Size Range	2.25 to 3.25 mm	3.25 to 3.75 mm	3.75 to 4.5 mm	4.5 to 5.5 mm	5.5 to 8 mm	8 mm and larger
Recommended Needle in U.S. Size Range	1 to 3	3 to 5	5 to 7	7 to 9	9 to 11	11 and larger
Approximate Yardage per 50 g Ball	180	150–160	125–135	70–100	50–55	35

Note: Different fiber content may offer different yardage per 50 grams; this chart gives averages. When unsure, always err on the side of buying too much yarn.

The following table gives approximate yardages needed for basic pullovers and cardigans in various sizes and weights of yarn. These estimates are for plain or lightly textured knitting. You will need more yarn—probably at least 25% or 30% more—for sweaters that have cable patterns and color work. Always buy more yarn than you think you will need and keep your receipts. Check with your local yarn store about their return policy. Many shops will allow you to return extra skeins of yarn for a refund or store credit for up to a year after your initial purchase.

Sweater Size	Fingering	Sport	DK	Worsted	Heavy Worsted	Bulky
Baby	350–600	300–500	280–500	260–450	220–380	170–300
Child	650–1125	550–950	500–925	500–840	400–700	320–550
Woman	1275–2400	1075–2025	1050–1975	950–1800	800–1500	625–1175
Man	1550–2600	1300–2200	1250–2150	1150–1950	975–1650	750–1250

BUTTONHOLE AND BUTTON BANDS

To calculate the number of stitches for a button or buttonhole band:

1. Measure the exact gauge of the stitch to be used in the bands.
2. Measure the length of the bands on the knitted pieces.
3. Multiply the gauge by the length to get the number of stitches to pick up.

EXAMPLE

You have lengthened a cardigan from what the pattern called for and you don't know how many stitches to pick up for the buttonhole band.

The bottom ribbing is the same ribbing you will be using for the buttonhole band.

The stitch gauge of the ribbing is 6 stitches per inch.

The length of your band is 17".

Multiply 17" by 6 stitches per inch, giving you 102 stitches.

Pick up 102 stitches for the button and buttonhole bands.

Buttonhole Spacing

Option 1:

- Make button band first.
- Place markers where buttons will be.
- On buttonhole band, make buttonholes to correspond to markers.

Option 2:

- Make button band first.
- Cut a piece of elastic half the length of your button band.
- Keeping the elastic unstretched, use a fine-point marker to make marks on the elastic in even intervals for the number of buttons you will be using.
- On button band, pin elastic at first mark for placement of top buttonhole.

- Stretch elastic so that last mark is in position of bottom buttonhole.
- Using pins or markers, mark buttonholes to correspond to marks on elastic.

Option 3:
- Subtract 1.5" from button-band length.
- Divide this length by the number of buttons minus one.
- Multiply this length by the stitch gauge of the button band to determine the number of stitches between each buttonhole.
- Make first and last buttonholes about ¾" from top or bottom of band.

EXAMPLE

Your button band is 17" long.

Gauge is 6 stitches per inch.

You have 7 buttons.

Length to make buttonholes is
17" – 1.5" = 15.5".

Divide 15.5 by 4 to get 3.875" between each buttonhole.

Multiply 3.875 by 6 stitches per inch to get 23 stitches between each buttonhole.

Remember that from this length of 23 stitches, a buttonhole must be made.

Glossary of Terms and Abbreviations

alt ....alternate

approx...approximately

beg...begin(ning)

BO ....bind off

CC ....contrast color

cm ....centimeters

cn ....cable needle

CO...cast on

cont..continue, continuing

ddec ....double decrease (decrease 2 stitches)

dec...decrease, decreasing

dinc..double increase (increase 2 stitches)

est..established

foll ....following

gauge..number of stitches and rows within a certain length measurement (also called tension)

inc ....increase, increasing

K ....knit

K2tog...Knit 2 stitches together (decrease 1 stitch).

K2tog tbl......................................Knit 2 stitches together through the back loop (decrease 1 stitch).

K3tog..Knit 3 stitches together (decrease 2 stitches).

knitwise...Work pattern in knit stitches.

left side ....left side of garment as you are wearing it

M1 ....Make 1 stitch (increase 1 stitch).

MC ....main color

mm..millimeters

P..purl

P2tog...Purl 2 stitches together (decrease 1 stitch).

P2tog tbl ....Purl 2 stitches together through the back loop (decrease 1 stitch).

patt(s)..pattern(s)

Pb..place bead

PM..place marker

psso...pass slipped stitch over

PU ....pick up and knit

purlwise...Work pattern in purl stitches.

rem...remain(ing)

rep ....repeat

rib...ribbing

right side ....right side of garment as you are wearing it

RS ....right side of knitting (side that will show when garment is worn)

sc ....single crochet (see page 27)

seed st (even number of sts):

....**Row 1:** *K1, P1*; rep from * to * to end of row.

....**Row 2:** *P1, K1*; rep from * to * to end of row.

selvage edge ....stitches that will be used for sewing

S2KP..Slip 2 stitches as if to K2tog, K1, pass slipped stitches over knit stitch (decrease 2 stitches).

Sl 1...Slip 1 stitch (unless otherwise stated, do this purlwise).

ssk...slip, slip, knit (decrease 1 stitch)

ssp...slip, slip, purl (decrease 1 stitch)

sssk..slip, slip, slip, knit (decrease 2 stitches)

st(s)...stitch(es)

St st...stockinette stitch: knit row 1, purl row 2

swatch...small piece of knitting used to determine gauge

tbl..through the back loop

tension...how tight the stitches and rows of knitting are (also called gauge)

tog..together

work even ....Work in established pattern without increasing or decreasing.

WS ....wrong side of knitting (side that will be on inside of garment when worn)

wyib ....with yarn in back of work

wyif ....with yarn in front of work

YO ....yarn over needle

Resources

Berroco
www.berroco.com
Chinchilla Bulky
Glacé
Suede
Ultra Alpaca

Blue Sky Alpaca
www.blueskyalpacas.com
Alpaca & Silk

The Great Adirondack Yarn Company
518-843-3381
e-mail psubik@nycap.rr.com
Silk Delight

Himalaya Yarn
www.himalayayarn.com
Recycled Silk

Karabella
www.karabellayarns.com
Gossamer

Laines Du Nord
www.knittingfever.com
Mulberry Silk

Louisa Harding Yarns
www.knittingfever.com
Impression
Kashmir Aran
Kimono Angora
Kimono Ribbon

Mountain Colors
www.mountaincolors.com
Twizzle

Noro
www.knittingfever.com
Silver Thaw

On Line
www.knittingfever.com
Clip

Plymouth Yarn
www.plymouthyarn.com
Baby Alpaca
Baby Alpaca D.K.
Baby Alpaca Grande
Bella Colour

Rowan
www.knitrowan.com
All Seasons Cotton
Summer Tweed

Trendsetter Yarns
www.trendsetteryarns.com
Segue

Knitting and Crochet Titles

CROCHET

Creative Crochet NEW!

Crochet for Babies and Toddlers

Crochet for Tots

Crochet from the Heart

Crocheted Socks!

Crocheted Sweaters

Cute Crochet for Kids NEW!

The Essential Book of Crochet Techniques

Eye-Catching Crochet

First Crochet

Fun and Funky Crochet

Funky Chunky Crocheted

Accessories NEW!

The Little Box of Crocheted Bags

The Little Box of Crocheted Hats and Scarves

The Little Box of Crocheted Ponchos and Wraps

More Crocheted Aran Sweaters

KNITTING

200 Knitted Blocks

365 Knitting Stitches a Year: Perpetual Calendar

Big Knitting

Blankets, Hats, and Booties

Dazzling Knits

Double Exposure

Everyday Style

Fair Isle Sweaters Simplified

First Knits

Fun and Funky Knitting

Funky Chunky Knitted Accessories

Handknit Style

Handknit Style II NEW!

Knits from the Heart

Knits, Knots, Buttons, and Bows

Knitted Shawls, Stoles, and Scarves

The Knitter's Book of Finishing Techniques

Lavish Lace

The Little Box of Knits for Baby NEW!

The Little Box of Knitted Ponchos and Wraps

The Little Box of Knitted Throws

The Little Box of Scarves

The Little Box of Scarves II

The Little Box of Sweaters

Modern Classics NEW!

Perfectly Brilliant Knits

The Pleasures of Knitting

Pursenalities

Pursenality Plus

Ribbon Style

Romantic Style

Sarah Dallas Knitting

Saturday Sweaters

Sensational Knitted Socks

Silk Knits NEW!

Simply Beautiful Sweaters

The Ultimate Knitted Tee

The Yarn Stash Workbook